SHELTON STATE COMMUNITY
    COLLEGE
JUNIOR COLLEGE
    LIBRARY

DISCARDED

hew

The CHURCH in SOVIET RUSSIA

THE CHURCH
IN SOVIET RUSSIA

BY MATTHEW SPINKA

GREENWOOD PRESS, PUBLISHERS
WESTPORT, CONNECTICUT

Library of Congress Cataloging in Publication Data

Spinka, Matthew, 1890-1972.
  The church in Soviet Russia.

    Reprint of the ed. published by Oxford University
  Press, New York.
    Bibliography: p.
    Includes index.
    1. Church and state in Russia--1917-   2. Orthodox
  Eastern Church, Russian--Russia--History--20th century.
  3. Russia--Church history--1917-   I. Title.
  [BR936.S62 1980]   322'.1'0947   80-18191
  ISBN 0-313-22658-X (lib. bdg.)

© Oxford University Press, Inc., 1956.

Reprinted with the permission of Oxford University Press, Inc.

Reprinted in 1980 by Greenwood Press
A division of Congressional Information Service, Inc.
88 Post Road West, Westport, Connecticut 06881

Printed in the United States of America

10 9 8 7 6 5 4 3 2 1

CONTENTS

INTRODUCTION

THE FALL of the Romanov dynasty in March 1917 had fateful consequences not only for the Russian state but for the Russian Orthodox Church as well. For the supreme administrative organization of the Church had been dominated by the tsar. Not that this subjection had been of the Church's choosing. It was Peter the Great who, in 1721, by his Ecclesiastical Regulations, had deprived the Church of the degree of autonomy it had enjoyed while it had been governed by its own Patriarchs. Peter had placed the Church under the administration of the Holy Governing Synod, composed of hierarchs appointed by himself. The tsars ever since had been represented in the Synod by the Ober-Procurator, and although this lay official had no vote, he nevertheless possessed enormous influence; for no action could be taken by the Synod and could receive the Emperor's approval without the Ober-Procurator's intermediation. The fall of the imperial regime, therefore, necessitated the reorganization of the supreme administration of the Russian Church.

The best hierarchs of that Church had long desired the restoration of the patriarchate. Ever since 1906, when the tsar consented to the calling of an All-Russian Sobor,* fifty of the most representative members of the Church had labored for a whole year upon the formulation of the problems to be discussed by, and the recommendations to be presented to, the Sobor. Their findings had been published in three large volumes (1906–7) and had testified to the sincere desire on the part of those representatives of the Church to abolish the Holy Governing Synod and restore the patriarchate. Unfortunately, the promised Sobor had not been held. Accordingly, when the Provisional Government gave the Church permission to hold a Sobor in 1917, the long-awaited opportunity to carry out the restoration of the patriarchate was at last at hand. It was this Sobor which actually realized the long-deferred hope.

Our interest centers in the relation of Church and state from the downfall of the tsarist regime and the subsequent October Revolution to the present (1955). Since such relations were most significantly displayed at the level of the Soviet government and the heads of the Church, the patriarchs, I have chosen to present the story of the modern Russian Orthodox Church in the form of an intensive study of the interaction of the Church with the state at this highest level. And although this pattern will not comprise all the facts which might be included in a chronological treatment of the subject, it is hoped that it will compensate for such omissions by other advantages, such as unified literary structure and the more complete development of the chosen subject. At any rate, no really important event will be omitted, as all such events had a necessary relation to the patriarch on the one hand and the state on the other.

---

* The term 'Sobor' means 'Council' in the ecclesiastical sense; since 'Soviet' likewise means 'Council,' I shall use the former term only for Russian ecclesiastical Councils.

Since the restored patriarchate was held by three occupants during the period under study, the present work will be divided into three main sections.

The first of the holders of the restored patriarchal office was Tikhon (1917–25); he was succeeded by Sergei (as deputy *locum tenens,* 1926–36, as *locum tenens,* 1936–43, and as patriarch, 1943–4); and the present occupant of the see is Alexei, who has held the office as *locum tenens,* 1944–5, and as patriarch from 1945 to date. As has already been indicated, our chief interest centers in the relation which these three supreme hierarchs of the Russian Orthodox Church have sustained toward the Soviet government. It is a tragic story of a gradual but inevitable subordination of the Church to the state in a manner not only resembling the worst days of tsarism but far exceeding them.

In Patriarch Tikhon's case, he at first refused to recognize the Soviet regime. He fought against it in both overt and passive fashions. But within a year he changed his policy and bent all his energies toward the task of securing for his Church an ecclesiastical autonomy within the framework of the state. With his arrest and imprisonment in 1922, and with the seizure of power in the Church by the schismatic groups which recognized the Soviet government, his efforts were defeated. The struggle was thus practically won by the regime. The defeat of Tikhon resulted in a radical change of his own policy. On that account, he was released the next year. Although he continued to hope that a *modus vivendi* might be worked out between the Church and the state whereby the former would receive legalization — and thus autonomy — his hopes were not realized. Before he died, Tikhon signed a document in which he yielded to the Soviet regime much of the freedom he so ardently tried to save for the Church; this was the price of regularizing the Church's relations with the state and thus gaining the legal right of administering the Church — a right denied the patriarch by the 1918 and subsequent Soviet legislation.

His successor, Metropolitan Sergei, continued these efforts. In 1927, he at last succeeded in gaining the desired recognition of himself and his Synod as the supreme administrators of the Church, but at a tremendous price. He thought it was worth it. For between 1922 and 1927, the patriarchal administration had been rendered practically impossible and thus the very existence of the Church seemed in jeopardy. It was under the pressure of such circumstances, and after he himself had been imprisoned, that Sergei capitulated and accepted the terms of the regime. But his personal act of submission, although taken in behalf of the Church, needed the approval of the Sobor of the whole Russian Church to make it canonical. Although Sergei himself specified this condition as absolutely necessary, no such approval has ever been given. Moreover, once Sergei submitted to the governmental control, he was obliged to subordinate the Church to the latter's interest to an ever greater degree. During the Second World War his subservience was so marked that at last even Stalin acknowledged the very great services rendered to the patriotic cause by the Church. He rewarded Sergei by allowing him to be elevated to the patriarchal throne.

Sergei's successor, the present Patriarch Alexei, has voluntarily and willingly continued the policy of co-operating with the state. He has deliberately made his Church a tool of the government. This is particularly evident from his services rendered to the state in the expansion of its political power into the satellite Orthodox countries. It has become the most significant and conspicuous feature of his term of office. Accordingly, at the present time, there exists but little opposition between the Church and the state in the Soviet Union. In its stead is to be plainly discerned a close co-operaton between the two bodies which amounts almost to an unequal partnership between them. The situation irresistibly reminds one of the tsarist period when a similar relation existed, with the exception that at the present time these two bodies are constitutionally separated, and that the government is officially non-religious, or even anti-religious. The state, on its part, gives substantial support to Alexei's ambition of supplanting the ecumenical patriarch of Constantinople as the *primus inter pares* among the Eastern Orthodox patriarchs. Thus the present state of the Russian Orthodox Church is, in many particulars, worse than ever before.

THE CHURCH IN SOVIET RUSSIA

I

Patriarch Tikhon's
Struggle for Church Autonomy

The first holder of the reorganized Russian patriarchate, Tikhon (1917–25), was born in 1866 in Toropets,
in the Pskov government, the son of the parish priest. His
secular name was Vasily Ivanovich Bellavin. The village
where he was born, and where his father served as priest
throughout his life, was famous for the ancient icon of the
Korsun Mother of God. This image is mentioned in the
earliest annals of Russian Christianity. Life in the village
was patriarchal, unaffected by modern currents; for it was
effectively cut off from the outside world, the nearest rail-
road being some two hundred versts distant.[1]

Young Vasily was destined to follow in his father's
priestly footsteps. Accordingly, after he had received his
elementary education in the village parochial school, he
entered in 1878 the Pskov Ecclesiastical Seminary, where
he remained for the next five years. His schoolmates remembered him as a tall, pale-complexioned youth of a
kindly, attractive, and genuinely pious disposition. He was
popular among them because he was not only a good student but was ever ready to help the less gifted, or perhaps
less industrious, fellow-students in time of trouble. Moreover, he was a jolly companion, not at all averse from a

good laugh. His popularity is attested by the nickname of 'archpriest' with which his schoolmates jokingly dubbed him.

When in 1883 he entered the St. Petersburg Theological Academy — a school of higher theological studies — his popularity there was signally attested in so far as his rank was jestingly raised by the students to that of 'patriarch.' When he actually reached that exalted office thirty-four years later, his former schoolmates often recalled their astounding foresight! This general favor in which young Bellavin was held is reflected in an incident recounted by his fellow-student, A. P. Rozhdestvensky, later professor at the St. Petersburg Academy: there existed, besides the official library of the Academy, a private student library, comprising mostly fiction and some 'forbidden' books. The student who was at the time in charge of this library was for some reason removed from his post by the rector. In protest, the entire student body refused to vote for anyone else but the deposed librarian. The rector then conceived the bright idea of suggesting Vasily Bellavin as the compromise candidate for the job. The suggestion was enthusiastically adopted by the students, and the revolt was ended.[2]

Since in the Eastern Orthodox Churches all hierarchical offices are reserved for monks,[3] it is customary for Academy students who aspire to these offices to profess the monastic vows in the fourth course, although some favorites make the profession earlier. But young Bellavin did not become a monk during his academic course. Instead, after his ordination, he was appointed to a teaching post at his own alma mater, the Pskov Seminary, where he taught theology. He remained there three years, and during that time earned for himself the affection of his students. But then unexpectedly, the young Seminary teacher applied to the local archpriest for the monastic cowl and soon after was 'shorn' by Bishop Germogen in the usual initiation ceremony to the monastic life. The rite, performed in the old Seminary church, was witnessed by a large crowd, the monk-novice having been known to them all his life. At this time he received the monastic name of Tikhon.

Thereupon, the young hieromonk served in various administrative capacities: he became at first the inspector, and later the rector, of the Kholm Seminary, located in a small town not far from the border of Austrian Galicia. His successor in this post, later Metropolitan Evlogy of Paris, characterized Tikhon as a 'good, jolly, kindly' person,[4] who greatly improved the Seminary. From this post Tikhon was elevated to the episcopal see of Lublin, having been consecrated bishop in 1897. In this capacity he served as vicar of the Kholm-Warsaw archdiocese. But the next year he was transferred to the United States, where he spent the subsequent nine years (1898–1907), administering the Russian churches scattered throughout the North American continent. In this position he succeeded Bishop Nikolai, along with whom he is regarded as the principal organizer of the present Russian Church in the United States. Since no other Orthodox Church administration existed in America at the time, Tikhon was called upon to care for other Orthodox communions besides his own. Thus, for instance, he administered the Syrian Antiochene diocese through his vicar-bishop, Raphael. This man was a Syrian, born in Damascus; but he had been educated at the Kazan Academy, and had been brought to the United States by Bishop Nikolai. Besides, Tikhon supervised the ecclesiastical affairs of such other churches as the Serbian, Greek, and Bulgarian Orthodox. At the time of his arrival, the episcopal see was located at San Francisco. Russian

Orthodoxy, first introduced into the Aleutian Islands and Alaska in the eighteenth century, in time had spread southward into California. In 1905, Tikhon transferred the headquarters to New York City, where the St. Nicholas Cathedral had been founded four years previously. The transfer was deemed necessary because the new Russian emigration, begun in the 1880's, was concentrated along the Atlantic seaboard. It consisted largely of Uniates from Austrian Galicia and the Sub-Carpathian region, hence not from Russia proper. Many of these people, dissatisfied with subjection to Roman Catholic superiors — mostly Irish — left Uniatism for Orthodoxy, and placed themselves under the jurisdiction of the Russian episcopacy. The vast Russian diocese was subdivided into two vicariates. In 1903, the Russian Orthodox Seminary opened its doors in Minneapolis, and the first Russian monastery, St. Tikhon's, was founded in Pennsylvania. During this period Tikhon visited Russia only once, when he was invited to take part in the summer session of the Holy Governing Synod. K. P. Pobedonostsev, who was then the Ober-procurator of the Holy Synod, soon discerned the outstanding administrative abilities of Bishop Tikhon and elevated him to the rank of 'Archbishop of Alaska and North America.' Before he left America, Tikhon elaborated a plan of constituting the American churches in an autonomous ecclesiastical body, independent of the Holy Governing Synod, for the majority of the Americans had never belonged to the Synod's jurisdiction, having come from the Austrian provinces. But the project remained unrealized during Tikhon's time.

In 1907, Tikhon was appointed to one of the oldest archdioceses in Russia, that of Yaroslavl. He soon gained popularity there by conducting tireless visitations throughout this extensive archdiocese, sometimes even on foot, and meeting the simple parish priests without any pretensions as to rank, in a kindly, person-to-person contact. No wonder that he was beloved by all his flock, clerical and lay alike.

But the Holy Governing Synod did not leave Tikhon to his congenial Yaroslavl see for long. After six years, he was transferred to a far more difficult post, the Vilna see in Russian Poland. The Yaroslavl city authorities honored him in a manner never before shown to any of his predecessors — by making him an honorary citizen of the town. In Vilna, Tikhon confronted a situation requiring skill and diplomacy; the Russians there were on terms of enmity with the predominant Polish population, so that the Russian hierarch needed to exercise extreme tact in order to avoid open conflict with the strongly Roman Catholic Poles. In this delicate task he proved himself unusually successful.

The First World War broke out while Tikhon was still in Vilna. This district became the scene of the earliest military operations between the Russian and the German armies, and a part of the archdiocese was occupied by the latter. Tikhon was forced to leave his see, and at first retired to Moscow, but later took up his residence in Disna, close to his archdiocese. He devoted himself to the spiritual care of the sick in the various military hospitals, for which service he was decorated. He likewise served as a member of the Holy Synod.

I

When the tsarist regime fell, in March 1917, and the Provisional Government took over, the post of the Ober-Procurator of the Holy Synod was occupied by V. N. Lvov.

Since the new government was predominantly liberal, the conservative body, such as the Holy Synod, was due for a thorough overhauling. During the February Revolution the Synod remained inactive; it refused even to condemn the revolutionary movement, as urged to do by the previous Ober-Procurator Raev.[5] On 4 March, the Synod even declared the revolution to be 'the will of God,' and substituted prayers for the Provisional Government in place of those for the tsar. Nevertheless, Lvov made known his intention to deprive all the existing synodical members of their posts and to create an entirely new Synod. Among the first to be expelled were Metropolitans Pitirim of St. Petersburg, Makary of Moscow, and Bishop Varnava of Tobolsk, notorious for their reactionary policies and their association with the ill-famed Rasputin. In April, Lvov made a clean sweep of the remaining members and the next day he announced the names of the new appointees. Only two members of the old Synod were reappointed — Archbishop Sergei of Vladimir, who in time succeeded Tikhon in the patriarchate, and Exarch Platon of Georgia. In fact, Sergei was named the head of the new body, and as such signed the call for the All-Russian Sobor to be held on 15 August.

But not only was the composition of the Synod 'liberalized'; there appeared the first sign of a far more radical movement within the Church, which in the end resulted in a serious schism. The center of this movement was Petrograd. It organized itself as the 'All-Russian Union of Democratic Orthodox Clergy and Laymen' on 20 March 1917. Its secretary, Archpriest Alexander Vvedensky, later became one of the leaders of the schismatic 'Living Church.'[6] These liberals went far beyond the rest of the Church in their demands for reforms, both ecclesiastical and economic. In some instances, their groups attempted to depose their bishops and to seize the administration of the archdioceses.

Since Archbishop Tikhon was without a diocese, having been driven out of Vilna by the Germans, he was eligible for another appointment. He was considered for the see of Petrograd, but was finally elected archbishop of Moscow, in succession to Makary, who had been pensioned. In that capacity he became the host of the All-Russian Sobor, which had been called to meet in Moscow. Among the new duties of Tikhon was the task of arranging for the accommodation of the numerous delegates to the Sobor. Moreover, since no such gathering had been held in Russia for some two-and-a-half centuries, it was no simple task to make proper and fitting preparations for the forthcoming event. It was this gathering which was charged with the long-desired and long-deferred task of reorganizing the administration of the Church by freeing it from subjection to the government. Many Church leaders — lay and clerical — hoped that this would mark the 'return of freedom' to the Church.[7]

The meetings of the Sobor were opened, on 15 August 1917, in the historic Uspensky Cathedral inside the walls of the Kremlin. The delegates numbered 564, and included all the diocesan bishops, comprising 10 metropolitans, 69 archbishops and bishops, 20 monks, 165 priests, deacons, and subdeacons, and 209 laymen, the rest being professors and officials. But the episcopal members alone had the right of passing finally on all legislation proposed by the whole body.[8] The opening ceremonies were conducted by the oldest of the hierarchs, Metropolitan Vladimir of Kiev, in the presence of Alexander Kerensky and other high-ranking members of the Provisional Government. When the Sobor got down to business, it was Tikhon, by that time raised to the rank of metropolitan, who was chosen to preside at the sessions. He was elected by a vote of 407 to 30 — a vote clearly reflecting the personal popularity he enjoyed.

The Sobor was soon divided into various parties of which the conservative, desiring the restoration of the patriarchate, was headed by the energetic, influential, and conservative Archbishop Antony (Khrapovitsky) of Kharkov, while the center was led by Prince Eugene N. Trubetskoy and Professor Sergei N. Bulgakov. The radically 'progressive' parties, represented largely by the professors from the Academies, favored a representative, synodal, form of government.

Although the Provisional Government treated the Church on the whole favorably, it was, after all, composed of liberals aiming at reforms. They intended to reform the Church as well. Thus, for instance, they hoped to effect, in course of time, the separation of Church and state. This intention the leaders of the Church resolutely opposed: they desired to obtain the support of the state without its interference in the autonomous administration of the Church. They also hoped to retain the privileges which the Church had enjoyed under the tsarist regime. Another cause of friction between the Church and the Kerensky government was the transfer of the 37,000 parochial schools — one-third of the total schools in the whole land — to the control of the Department of Education. Even the 'liberals' among the clergy opposed it. The government likewise made the compulsory religious instruction in public schools optional. It is clear that the Sobor would have come to blows with the Provisional Government had the latter retained power. This latent tension also explains the favorable attitude given by the Sobor to the bid for support made by General Kornilov in his unsuccessful attempt to overthrow the Kerensky regime in August 1917,[9] although the Sobor took no definite action in his support.

But the principal task of the Sobor concerned the form which the supreme administration of the Church was to take: was it to be patriarchate, as the party of Archbishop Antony advocated, or a Synod composed of elected representatives of the entire Church, as the moderates and the liberals strove for? The debate was long and heated. The Synodal party at first seemed to possess the majority. But the peasant lay members joined the patriarchal party and thus swung the vote in favor of the restoration of the patriarchate. Moreover, the decisive change in the sentiment of the Sobor occurred when the Bolsheviks, having decided to seize the government, staged the attack on the Petrograd Winter Palace and the Admiralty by shelling them from the warship *Aurora* (25 October o.s.). Soon a similar conflict broke out in Moscow, where the Kremlin, held by the 'cadets,' was besieged by the Bolsheviks. This caused a panic among the members of the Sobor, who feared that once the Kremlin fell to the besiegers, the Sobor would be dispersed without accomplishing its chief purpose. These events also strengthened the argument of the patriarchal party which urged that in the disturbed state of the country a strong man was needed to head the Church and defend its interests. Hence, although the debate was far from finished — there were still fifty speakers to be heard from — the discussion was terminated. It was Paul Grabbe who, five days after the fall of the Provisional Government, made the motion that the patriarchate be restored, although not with the old, autocratic powers. The supreme legislative, administrative, and judicial powers were declared to be the prerogatives of the All-Russian Sobor composed of bishops, clergy, and laymen. The patriarch was the head of the administration of the Church between the sessions of the Sobor, but could make no decisions independently of the Holy Synod and the Supreme Church Council which were associated with him, and of which he was the permanent chairman. Both he and the two associated bodies were responsible to the Sobor.

The vote on this momentous question was taken on 30 October: a comparatively small number of delegates participated, for the street fighting in the vicinity of the Kremlin kept many of them away. One of the members of the Sobor, Prince Gregory Trubetskoy, left a graphic account of the difficulty with which he and his brother, the philosopher Eugene Trubetskoy, reached the meeting. They had hardly passed a certain street when shots were exchanged between the two groups of fighters. At one place they had to place a ladder against a wall and climb over it.[10] Furthermore, not all those who were present took part in the voting: of the 317 members present, only 265 voted, 141 for and 112 against; consequently, less than half of the total number of delegates (564) participated in the most important decision affecting the future of the Russian Orthodox Church.

When the mode of the patriarchal election came up for consideration, it was Professor Sokolov's suggestion that prevailed. He advocated the plan of electing twenty-five candidates from among the bishops, priests, and laymen. Of these, by a further selection, three nominees were chosen: on the first ballot Archbishop Antony (Khrapovitsky) of Kharkov, the leader of the party advocating the restoration of the patriarchate, received the largest number of votes (101); and Archbishop Arseny of Novgorod and Metropolitan Tikhon of Moscow were next in line (27 and 23 respectively). After two other ballots, the bishops, instead of assuming the responsibility for the selection of the patriarch from among the three nominees — as was their right — relinquished their privilege in favor of leaving the selection to the 'divine will,' i.e. to the choice by lot. This solemn ceremony took place on 5/18 November, in the magnificent Church of Christ the Saviour (which later was torn down to make room for the House of the Soviets, the erection of which has since been abandoned). The oldest hieromonk, Alexei, drew from the urn which had been placed in front of the icon of the Vladimir Mother of God — brought for that purpose from the Uspensky cathedral — one of the three slips inscribed with the names of the nominees. He handed it to Metropolitan Vladimir, who then solemnly intoned: 'Tikhon, the Metropolitan of Moscow.' [11] The newly elected patriarch was then enthroned, on 29 November, in the Uspensky cathedral, despite the fact that the Kremlin had in the meantime fallen into the hands of the Bolsheviks. But they interfered neither with the enthronization ceremony nor with the meetings of the Sobor. Tikhon occupied the patriarchal throne which had been preserved from the days of Peter the Great. He was clad in the splendid robes of the former patriarchs, holding the scepter of Metropolitan Peter and wearing the headdress and the mantle of Patriarch Nikon.

The election of Tikhon could hardly be said to have 'satisfied everybody,' as Prince Trubetskoy asserted.[12] In fact, it was a great disappointment both to Archbishop Antony and his party and to the 'liberals' who wanted to set up a synodical form of administration. Had the usual method of election been followed instead of the mode by lot, there is little, if any, doubt that Antony or Arseny would have been chosen, more likely the former, who had received the largest number of votes among the three can-

didates. Moreover, Antony possessed the qualities of the
'strong' man desired for the post in view of the disturbed
state of affairs — qualities which Tikhon lacked. For that
reason, the Sobor chose 'strong' men as members of the
Holy Synod, composed of twelve bishops, and of the Supreme Church Council, comprising fifteen members chosen
from among the bishops, clergy, and laymen, with whose
advice Tikhon was to administer the Church.

But Tikhon was likewise faced with the hostility and
opposition within the ranks of the parochial clergy. The
recently organized 'Union of Democratic Orthodox Clergy
and Laymen' now definitely repudiated the patriarch and
extended its propaganda in behalf of synodical administration and other reforms from Petrograd, where the movement centered, into such important provincial centers as
Kiev and Odessa. Even though the opposition was as yet
weak and limited to a relatively small priestly party, in
course of time it almost succeeded in abolishing the patriarchate and making itself supreme in the Church.[13]

II

The inevitable conflict between the newly elected Patriarch and the Bolshevik regime broke out scarcely two
months later. The Bolshevik attitude toward religion in
general, and the Russian Orthodox Church in particular,
was no secret. Lenin made repudiation of all religion a
dogma. The official philosophical spokesman for the Party
(put to death as a traitor during the purges of 1936-8),
N. Bukharin, wrote in 1918: 'The working class and its
Party, the Party of Communists-Bolsheviks, strives not only
for economic liberation, but along with it for spiritual liberation of the toiling masses.' [14] Accordingly, the first legis-

lative act of the new government, written by Lenin during the first night after the seizure of power and passed by the *Sovnarkom* the next day, declared that 'The right of private ownership of land is abolished forever . . . All land — state appanage, cabinet, monastery, church, entail, private, communal, peasant, and any other lands, passes to the nation without indemnification and is turned over for the use of those who till it . . .' [15] The Church was thus stripped of its property literally overnight. Other similar acts of spoliation, such as the legalization of civil marriage, followed shortly thereafter and created hostility against the regime on the part of the Church leaders. In January 1918, when it became known that the regime was preparing the basic law of separation of Church and state and Church and school, Tikhon, without waiting either for the publication of the law or for the reconvening of the Sobor (which was recessed for the Christmas holidays), went into action. He issued, on 19 January, a strongly worded condemnation of the acts already passed by the Soviets, such as the secularization of marriage and the nationalization of schools, the confiscation of Church property, and various acts of desecration of churches and monasteries. He called it 'a satanic act, for which you shall suffer the fire of Gehenna in the life to come, beyond the grave, and terrible curses of posterity in this present, earthly life.' He thereupon forbade those guilty of such deeds to come 'to the sacraments of Christ' and summarily anathematized them. Furthermore, he adjured the faithful 'not to commune with such outcasts of the human race in any manner whatsoever.' [16]

This was a veritable flaunting of the patriarchal gauntlet in the face of the Soviet government, a defiance which marshalled the forces of Church and state into a warlike array. When the Sobor reconvened a few days later, it

wholeheartedly approved the Patriarch's declaration and
added to it some harsh and uncompromising statements of
its own. It may perhaps be difficult to conceive of such a
direct challenge to the government on the part of the
Church. But one must remember that at that time it was
by no means certain whether the Bolsheviks would retain
their power. They themselves had officially styled their
regime as 'provisional,' for the permanent government was
to be formed only after the Constitution was adopted. This
was to be done by the Constitutional Assembly which met
in the Tauride Palace in Petrograd on 18 January 1918.
The Bolsheviks, of course, hoped that they would have
majority at this democratically elected Assembly, and thus
secure legal basis for their revolutionary government. But
the results of the election, which had been held on 25
November 1917, had been deeply disappointing to them: of
the 36 million votes cast, only 9 million (25 per cent) had
favored the Bolsheviks, while 21 million electors (about
58 per cent) had cast their votes for the Social Revolutionary Party. Even so, the Bolshevik leaders, hoping for some
miracle, desperately clung to the possibility of securing the
domination over the Assembly when it actually met in
January. Their hopes were utterly frustrated: a Social
Revolutionary, Victor Chernov, was elected president by
a large majority. Thereupon, Lenin allowed the Assembly
to hold its session throughout the day and up to 5 a.m. of
the next day. During this first and only session, the Assembly succeeded in proclaiming Russia a Federated Republic,
and in transferring all land to the peasants. But the next
day the delegates found the gates of the palace closed and
barred by troops armed with rifles and machine guns. The
same day Lenin issued a decree stating: 'The Constituent
Assembly is dissolved. The Soviet Revolutionary Republic

will triumph, no matter what the cost.' [17] Henceforth, his regime no longer styled itself 'provisional.' These events, which transpired at the very time when Tikhon issued his challenge to the Soviet regime, afford at least a partial explanation of the Patriarch's and the Sobor's conviction that Lenin's regime could not last long.

Nor were the forces that the Church could muster in its defense negligible. There were some 71,000 priests and monks, and some 117 million members of the Church. The hold of the clergy upon the masses, particularly upon the peasantry, was still formidable, although fluctuating. By organizing brotherhoods and conducting street demonstrations, the Church could exert powerful influence against the new masters of Russia.

To be sure, the government did not altogether ignore the challenge. There were rumors that the *Sovnarkom* intended to 'make an end of Tikhon.' Members of the Holy Council of the Sobor were sufficiently alarmed that they actually elected, in a secret session, several 'deputies' of the Patriarch, so that in case Tikhon should be arrested, they could succeed him one after another. When the Patriarch was told of this action, he remarked with a smile: 'So they buried me alive!' [18] Trotsky, who was at the time the leading member of the governmental committee for ecclesiastical affairs, demanded Tikhon's punishment. But Lenin and Bonch-Bruevich prevailed against Trotsky, urging that 'it is dangerous to touch that priest.' Trotsky succeeded only in having Tikhon put under house arrest. All through this hubbub, the Patriarch remained calm and unperturbed.

Nevertheless, the government was ready to act. Five days after Tikhon's proclamation it published its basic ecclesiastical legislation, ['The Law of Separation of Church and

State and School and Church.' [19] The law was closely mod-
elled on the analogous French law passed in 1905. The
Church was separated from the state, but the 'free performance of religious rites [was] guaranteed as long as it did not
interfere with public order.' Furthermore, the school was
separated from the Church, and religion could be taught
only in a private manner to children in groups of not more
than three. All properties of the Church were declared 'to
form national wealth,' and the right to possess property on
the part of the Church was declared illegal. Religious associations were likewise deprived of the rights of juridical
persons. Nevertheless, if they were organized in accordance
with the specific regulations issued by the government, they
could apply for the 'free' use of the church buildings. But
the support of the clergy had to be voluntary, not compulsory.

The ultimate aim of this legislation, as even Julius
Hecker, a writer well disposed to the Soviet regime (later
he became a member of the Communist Party) admits, 'was
to destroy the Church altogether and to eradicate religion
from the hearts and minds of the people.' [20] The means to
that end are easily discernible in the Law of Separation,
even though all its provisions could not be put into effect
immediately. First of all, the Church was deprived of all
its property and thrown on the voluntary support of the
equally impoverished lay people. The extent of the land
lost by the Church was estimated at 4 million desyatins (a
desyatin equals 2.7 acres) and all other forms of wealth lost
by it amounted to 8 billion rubles. Besides, it lost the an-
nual state subsidy of 35 million rubles.[21] Moreover, its centralized, hierarchical administration was deprived by law
of its control over the parishes, which were then organized
only locally, congregationally, under lay control. In course

of time this threatened to put an end to the very existence of the Church. And finally, by secularizing the parochial schools and forbidding religious instruction to youth under eighteen years of age, except in groups of three, the extinction of the Church was envisaged in no distant future.

But soon the government was involved in the peace negotiations with the German forces on its western border which resulted in the disastrous Brest-Litovsk Peace. Patriarch Tikhon had the courage — or audacity — to condemn it. Besides, the government was engaged in a civil war with the various White armies in the South and the Siberian Provisional Government which was set up by the former members of the Constituent Assembly. During this civil strife, the former Imperial family, held in prison at Ekaterinburg, was brutally exterminated on 16 July. Tikhon declared in the Kazan Cathedral that the murder of the tsar, who had abdicated and had since made no attempt to interfere in the political life of the country, was a heinous crime and 'whoever does not condemn it, will be guilty of his blood.' Moreover, he boldly celebrated, together with members of the Sobor, a requiem mass for the unfortunate victims in the Church of the Archdiocesan House.[22] This defiant act certainly did not help the relations between the Church and the state. Nevertheless, for the time being the government ignored it, although the Patriarch received soon after a summons to appear before the Soviet officials. But he disregarded the request. On its part, the government adopted its first Constitution in July 1918, wherein article 13 repeated the provisions of the January law by stating: 'In order to guarantee to workers actual freedom of conscience, the Church is separated from the government and the school from the Church; and the liberty of religious as well as of anti-religious propaganda is granted to all citizens.' [23]

Obviously, Patriarch Tikhon played what seemed a dangerous game; for if the Soviet regime should retain its hold on the helm of the state, he was certain to be crushed by its might. Many of the members of the Sobor tried to prevent such consequences for the Patriarch by urging him to leave Moscow and to take refuge elsewhere, perhaps even abroad. But Tikhon resolutely refused: 'The flight of the Patriarch,' he replied, 'would play into the hands of the enemies of the Church; they would exploit it for their purposes. Let them do as they see fit.' [24] And despite this known danger to his safety, Tikhon, in October 1918, when the regime was busy with preparations for the first anniversary of the Revolution, was the only person who dared to pen a declaration, 'the strongest of anything that he has hitherto written against Bolshevism.' [25] Even his own advisers were frightened. But Tikhon sent it directly to Lenin on the eve of the celebration. It is a marvel that the latter did not take decisive measures against the Patriarch. All that the regime did was to place him under house arrest, but refrained from further molestation. Tikhon lived in the modest establishment of the Trinity *podvorye,* belonging to the Trinity-Sergei monastery. Three Red Army soldiers were quartered on the lower floor to keep him under surveillance, but he was free to move about in the little enclosure surrounding the house. Nevertheless, having been registered as a 'bourgeois,' he was classed, along with his clergy, as belonging to 'non-productive elements' and denied a ration card. He received his food from his parishioners. Likewise, they provided him with a bodyguard of eighteen unarmed men who served for a week at a time.

Under such circumstances, the conflict of the Soviet government with the Church was inevitable: it at first took the form of persecution of the hierarchs and the clergy. The ancient and historic churches in the Kremlin were closed, and the relics of the great Russian saints kept in the Cathedral of the Assumption, the most famous of them, were destroyed. The same procedure was followed in Petrograd with the relics of St. Alexander Nevsky, and in Zadonsk with the remains of St. Tikhon. Some of the relics were placed in museums, and a wide publicity was given them. Printing establishments of the Trinity-Sergei monastery and of the Holy Synod in Moscow were confiscated, and all Church publications discontinued. The second method of conflict with the Church was that of depriving it of organized leadership. Twenty-eight hierarchs were murdered: Metropolitan Vladimir of Kiev was brutally killed in January 1918; Archbishop Vasily of Chernigov, Bishop Andronik of Perm, who was bestially tortured, Bishop Germogen of Saratov, Bishop Ephraim of Irkutsk, and Bishop Pimen were also murdered. Thousands of clerics of all ranks were thrown into prisons without any trial, and twelve thousand others were reported by the *émigré* press as put to death.[26]

There can be no doubt that during the first year of his administration Tikhon used his office for political opposition to the Bolshevik regime, as under the circumstances was not difficult to understand. But he soon recognized that the policy hitherto pursued by him and his Synod was wrong. His essential greatness may be seen in the fundamental change of his orientation which occurred either during the summer of 1918, as Fedotov asserts,[27] or during 1919, as Stratonov claims.[28] Both assert that Tikhon assumed an 'a-political,' neutral relation to the state, although it also involved him in recognition of the Soviet regime as the legal government of the country to which civil obedience is due. This new policy was based on a strict interpretation of the Constitution, which separated the Church from the state, by reason of which the Church should have enjoyed freedom and autonomy in its internal administration. This fundamental change in the ecclesiastical orientation was facilitated by the fact that the elements in the Church — both lay and clerical — most strongly opposed to the Soviet regime had joined the White armies or other anti-Bolshevik military forces engaged in the Civil War and, with their eventual defeat, had left the country in the wake of the defeated armies. Those that remained in the Soviet Union were therefore, by and large, inclined to the new policy of political non-intervention. Once more the cry arose within the Church: 'Let us withdraw into the catacombs!' The Patriarch, who became the personification of this policy, therefore requested the parishes and the clergy 'not to bring politics into the Church.' Stratonov asserts that 'The political activity of church functionaries which had been carried on hitherto, was from that moment completely stopped. The request of the Patriarch was fulfilled with remarkable consistency by the entire Church body; particularly the hierarchs and the clergy gave up politics, and devoted all their endeavors to the service of the Church which at that time required extreme effort. The lay people co-operated in this without any special agreement. Politicians ceased to be active in politics. Having abandoned social activity, both groups became more devoted than formerly to the Church and to preserve among themselves most sincere and satisfactory relations.' [29] Although such near-absolute statements are contradicted by undoubted acts of co-operation of the clergy with the White armies or Kolchak's Siberian government, they may be accepted as representing the Patriarch's intention. He likewise refused to send his blessings to General Denikin, the leader of the Whites.

Moreover, many priests who had been in prison were now released and returned to their parishes (1920). As so often happens during religious persecution, there occurred a religious awakening among the masses. Churches were filled and among the attendants was a larger proportion of men than ever before. 'There is no doubt,' reports Stratonov, 'that the inner growth of religious consciousness of the Russian faithful reached heights such as did not exist for the last two centuries of Russian ecclesiastical life.' [30]

But such was not the understanding of the Law of Separation on the part of the Soviet leaders: they adhered to the dictum that 'he who is not with us, is against us.' Accordingly, they would be satisfied with nothing less than the complete and positive support of their policy by the Church. Consequently, the disorganization of the central administration of the Church resulting from the attacks of the government upon the episcopal leadership was so great that it caused Patriarch Tikhon to take a radical step to counter it. With the approval of the Holy Synod and the Supreme Church Council, he issued an *Ukaz* (7 Nov. 1920), granting each diocesan bishop the right to administer his diocese or archdiocese independently of the central patriarchal administration, until such time as the bishops would have free access and intercourse with the latter.[31] After Tikhon's arrest this decision was repeated in the circular sent to the entire Russian episcopate by the patriarchal *locum-tenens*, Metropolitan Agathangel of Yaroslavl (5/18 June 1922):

Beloved in the Lord, most holy hierarchs, temporarily deprived of supreme leadership: administer your archdioceses independently, in accordance with the Holy Writ and the holy canons; and until the restitution of the Supreme Church government decide definitely all affairs about which formerly you were wont to request the decision of the Holy Synod.[32]

These actions resulted in a virtual autonomy of the archdioceses both within the Soviet Union and abroad.

With the defeat of the White armies in southern Russia, many officers and men of this now utterly dispirited band sought refuge abroad. Along with them, as has already been noted, went many clerical and hierarchical opponents of Bolshevism, some of whom were monarchical restorationists. These refugees found cordial welcome in Yugoslavia, where the episcopal members of this group organized themselves into the Supreme Russian Ecclesiastical Administration Abroad, with Metropolitan Antony of Kiev and Kharkov, the defeated candidate for the patriarchate, at their head. This group held a conference at Karlovtsi in November 1921, which was attended by a large number of formerly high-placed politicians, most of them strongly conservative. Among them was the president of the last Duma, M. V. Rodzyanko, who was influential in securing Tsar Nicholas' resignation. He had also been an active member of the Sobor of 1917–18. But the monarchist lay elements protested against him and secured his voluntary withdrawal from the membership. His exclusion was sanctioned by Antony.

The declaration prepared before the Conference convened asserted positively that the hierarchical members regarded themselves as subject to the supreme authority of the Moscow Patriarch, and that all decisions must be approved by him before they were to have final validity.

However, by the time the Conference met, the mood of the participants had changed: this was apparent in the committee appointed to formulate a resolution about 'the spiritual revival of Russia,' the chairman of which was Archbishop Anastasy, later the successor of Antony as the head of the Karlovtsi group. Its outstanding lay member, N. E. Markov, belonged to the monarchical faction bent upon utilizing the Conference for political ends. They proposed the inclusion of a phrase regarding the restoration of the Romanov dynasty to the Russian throne. Archbishop Anastasy objected to it on the ground that the Conference should not deal with politics; but he was outvoted. When the resolution finally reached the floor of the Conference, 34 members opposed the phrase on the same ground as Anastasy, but refrained from final voting. Thus the resolution was adopted by a vote of 51, among whom only one-half of the hierarchs (6) and 7 clerics voted for it, while the remaining 38 were laymen. The offending political phrase read: 'And may [the Lord God] return to the all-Russian throne His Anointed, strong in the love of the nation, the lawful Orthodox tsar of the House of Romanov.' [33] It was this unfortunate resolution which enormously aggravated the already extremely difficult situation of the Church in Russia. As Stratonov evaluates its effect, 'The results of the work of the ecclesiastical gathering as expressed in the adoption of that message were harmful to the émigré ecclesiastical circles, and became wholly tragic to the Mother-Church. It would be difficult to show throughout the whole course of Church history another such disastrous event.' [34]

Moreover, Metropolitan Antony suggested (on 1 December) that the Conference be designated as a Sobor, thus raising its authority to an equality with the most important

ecclesiastical gatherings (such, for instance, as that of 1917–
18). When this suggestion was adopted, the 'Sobor', still
under the predominant influence of the lay monarchist
party, instructed the newly organized Supreme Church Administration to address a memorial to the Genoa Conference, then in session. The Sobor asked the conference to
exclude the Soviet delegates from attendance, and to provide arms to the 'honorable Russian citizens' and 'help
them to drive Bolshevism — this cult of killing, looting,
and blasphemy — out of Russia.' [35] This appeal had no
effect on the struggle with the Soviet government, but
'played the role of a hammer and an anvil' as far as the
Russian Church was concerned. '

The government promptly seized this opportunity to
charge Tikhon with responsibility for the treasonable conduct of the Karlovtsi hierarchs, and as early as February
cited him to appear and answer the charge. When the
Novoe Vremya of Belgrade published the Karlovtsi resolution on 1 March 1922, Patriarch Tikhon wrote to the
leaders abroad for an explanation and confirmation. Their
replies were negative. Thereupon, he submitted the case to
the Holy Synod and the Supreme Ecclesiastical Council,
along with them relieved the Karlovtsi hierarchs of their
offices, and declared on 22 April/3 May that since the
refugee hierarchs had no right to speak in behalf of the
Russian Orthodox Church, their pronouncement did not
'represent the official voice of the Russian Orthodox
Church, and in view of their political character, did not
possess ecclesio-canonical character.' Furthermore, he categorically liquidated the Karlovtsi Church Administration.
At the same time he transferred the administration of all
Russian Orthodox churches in Western Europe to Metropolitan Evlogy, who had his headquarters in Paris.[36] Thus

Tikhon clearly cut himself from the monarchist politics abroad.

The situation was further complicated when in the fall of 1921 a famine of unprecedented proportions broke out. In August the Patriarch appealed for help both to his own flock, the other Orthodox patriarchs, and the Pope, the Archbishop of Canterbury, and the Episcopal Bishop of New York. The General Committee for the Aid of the Starving, appointed by the government, asked Tikhon for his co-operation. He organized a special All-Russian Church Committee for the purpose of conducting collections in the parishes. But later the authorities declared this committee superfluous, and took over the funds collected by it. The order was complied with. Early in 1922, when information about the anti-Soviet resolutions passed by the Karlovtsi 'Sobor' began to reach the Soviet Union, the mood of the government changed for the worse. The regime seized upon this famine occasion to open its campaign against the Church. It began considering the confiscation of Church valuables. On 16 February the regime announced its decision to remove the valuables 'as far as the removal would not interfere with the cultus itself.' The Patriarch issued, on 19 February, instructions to the parishes, allowing them to donate such church ornaments as possessed no liturgical significance, making a distinction between 'consecrated' and 'unconsecrated' objects. But on 26 February, the government ordered the removal of 'all valuable objects of gold, silver and precious stones . . . which cannot actually interfere with the interests of the cult itself . . . ,' [37] thus ignoring the distinction previously made by the Patriarch between the 'consecrated' and 'unconsecrated' articles of liturgical use. Thereupon, three days later, Tikhon issued a proclamation in which he pointed out this non-recognition by the decree of the all-important distinction, and declared:

From the point of view of the Church, such an act is sacreligious, and we esteem it our sacred duty to make known the view of the Church regarding the act and to inform our faithful children about it.[38]

Thereupon, he once more instructed the clergy to surrender any objects which had not been consecrated, but forbade as uncanonical the voluntary surrender of any consecrated object. Penalty for such an action for laymen was excommunication; for clergy, deprivation of their sacerdotal rank. In this, he acted in accordance with the ruling of the Sobor of 1918, which declared confiscation of 'holy things' as blasphemous.[39]

On 15 March *Izvestiya* published an interview with the Patriarch in which his stand was reported without as yet denouncing or attacking him therefor. Between 17 and 25 March the collection of church valuables got under way. The faithful were now 'between the devil and the deep sea' — the governmental and patriarchal orders. In some places — Shuya, Moscow, Leningrad, Smolensk, and others — the governmental action resulted in popular riots, with consequent numerous arrests. Elsewhere there was no opposition. The first article denouncing the Church for its opposition to the order appeared in *Izvestiya* on 28 March under the caption 'The Most Holy Counter-Revolution.' The Church was charged with collusion with the Karlovtsi 'Sobor' and with the exploitation of the famine as a means of overthrowing the government. This charge was given color by the publicly expressed hopes of the Karlovtsi emigrés that such would be the effect of the famine. Protopriest G. Shavelsky, the former chief chaplain of the Russian Army, wrote an article expressing the sentiment, and even suggesting that the debacle caused by the famine might give the Patriarch an opportunity to pass on the power to 'the lawful bearer of that power.' [40] The government charged Tikhon with secretly sharing that sentiment and acting accordingly.

The removal of sacred objects from the churches resulted in outbreaks of violence on the part of the faithful, and consequently in arrests and trials. There were 231 trials of those arrested for obstructing the execution of the order, in which 738 accused were examined and 44 were sentenced to death. The Petrograd and Moscow trials were most widely publicized. In the former city, death penalty was imposed on ten (later reduced to four) of the accused, among them the popular and beloved Metropolitan Benjamin. He was arrested for his opposition to the Living Church's usurpation of the patriarchal office by its leaders—Vvedensky, Krasnitsky, Belkov, and others. Benjamin thereupon had excommunicated Vvedensky. It was because of this opposition that he was put on trial. Vvedensky and Krasnitsky testified against him. As a result he was sentenced to death. [41] In Moscow, the prosecutor declared: 'We do not judge the Church [as a whole], but the individuals who used the legal forms of the ecclesiastical apparatus for an underground attack on the Soviet government.' [42] Even the Patriarch was cited as a witness at this trial, but denied any direct knowledge of the Karlovtsi decisions. After fourteen hours of deliberation the death penalty was passed upon eleven defendants and the rest were sentenced to prison terms ranging from one to five years. Among those sentenced to death were the Roman Catholic Archbishop Tseplyak and Vicar-General Budkevich; both received the death sentence, but only the latter was actually executed. [43]

But the Soviet authorities were bent on far more decisive

policies in regard to the Church and the Patriarch, and the latter's condemnation of the Karlovtsi Sobor was insufficient to appease them. They desired to condemn Tikhon himself by implicating him in treasonable counter-revolutionary activity, and perhaps putting him to death.

Therefore, when the group of 'progressive' clergy decided to seize the administration of the Church by securing the removal of the Patriarch from his office, this scheme fitted well with the desires of the government and received its support. Representatives of this group of 'white' clergy visited Tikhon on 12 May, and apparently convinced him that his arrest was imminent. For two days later he appointed Metropolitan Agathangel of Yaroslavl as his *locum tenens* and asked him to come to Moscow without delay. He instructed him to call the second All-Russian Sobor which was to decide upon the policies to be pursued and either approve or reject his (Tikhon's) conduct of affairs. After his release from prison, Tikhon asserted that he had been granted the approval of the government for these acts. But Agathangel at first delayed to act upon the Patriarch's instructions, and later he was prevented by the regime from leaving his see. Moreover, he himself was soon arrested and sent into exile to the Narym territory.

The leaders of the 'progressive' clergy, whose organization assumed the name of the Living Church, did not allow grass to grow under their feet. Two days after their first visit to Tikhon they, together with Bishop Antonin who joined them, published in *Izvestiya* an appeal to the faithful. In it they echoed the charges of the government by accusing the leaders of the Church of an attempt to overthrow the government. They furthermore announced that they had already turned to the regime requesting that they be permitted to call 'a Sobor for the trial of the guilty and the solution of the question of ecclesiastical administration,' [44] i.e. they requested recognition as the official heads of the Church. The proclamation was signed by Bishop Antonin and the Leningrad priests Kalinovsky, Krasnitsky, Vvedensky, Belkov, and psalmsinger Stadnikov; with them were associated Moscow priests Borisov and Bykov and Saratov archpriests Rusakov and Ledovsky — ten members of the 'white clergy' altogether, besides the one bishop.

Thus curiously enough, this 'leftist' pro-Soviet group formed within the Russian Church on the Soviet territory, agreed with the rightist and monarchist party among the *émigrés* in opposing Tikhon's neutral stand — except that they would have the Patriarch support actively the Soviet brand of politics rather than the monarchist kind.

On 18 May, this group, consisting of priests Vvedensky, Belkov, and Kalinovsky, visited Tikhon once more and presented him with a written request demanding that they be allowed to carry on the routine work of the chancery until Metropolitan Agathangel should arrive. Tikhon, quite unaware of the ultimate aims and plans of his petitioners, yielded to this request, but clearly specified that they were to relinquish the work to Agathangel as soon as he should arrive. He moreover committed the administration of the Moscow archdiocese to Bishop Innokenty of Klin, and until his arrival, temporarily to Bishop Leonid. Thereupon the Living Church leaders, with the aid of the regime, proceeded to seize control of the patriarchal office, not merely of the chancery.[45] After the Patriarch was transferred from the house arrest in the Trinity *podvorye* to the GPU prison (5 August 1922), the usurpers felt that they had a free hand, and that Tikhon would never trouble them again. Stratonov declares that 'from that moment begins the ecclesiastical cleavage of the Russian Orthodox flock.' [46] The usurping group went so far as to claim that they had Tikhon's authorization for their act. On one occasion, when someone suggested that the Patriarch's approval for a certain measure was needed, Bishop Antonin declared: 'As Patriarch Tikhon has transmitted his authority to the Supreme Ecclesiastical Administration without reservations, we have no need to run after him to receive from him what he no longer possesses.' [47]

Once in control, the usurping party took measures to secure its hold upon the Church by elevating a large number of its adherents — mostly of the parochial clergy — to positions of influence and power. On 29 May they called a conference which adopted a party program and organized as the new Church authority the Supreme Ecclesiastical Administration. It was headed by Bishop Antonin, who had been in retirement, but now assumed active administrative duties without patriarchal authorization. Bishop Leonid, appointed by Tikhon to administer the Moscow archdiocese, likewise went over to the schismatics. Besides the two bishops, the Supreme Administration was composed of priests Vladimir Krasnitsky and Alexander Vvedensky.

The Living Church party clearly intended to transfer the administration of the Russian Church from that of the monastic episcopate to that of the 'white' parochial clergy. This then was a radical 'priestly' revolt against the age-long but canonically-required exclusive rule of the monastic episcopate, for the membership of the Living Church was overwhelmingly priestly. The party aimed even at abandoning the patriarchal form of government altogether and substituting for it the synodical pattern, in which the priestly element would predominate. Moreover, the party condemned the Patriarch's abstention from politics and demanded an active participation of the Church in the 'socialist upbuilding.' Stratonov designates the party as 'the priestly reaction against the reforms effected by the legislation of the All-Russian Sobor of 1917–18,' [48] while Professor Titlinov — one of the outstanding representatives of the later party of the Renovators — calls it 'not a reforming but a revolutionary movement.'

After the Conference, a delegation of the Living Church visited Metropolitan Agathangel in Yaroslavl, trying to win him to the new regime in the Church. He refused. But henceforth at least he no longer remained inactive: he issued a statement urging the faithful to guard the unity of the Church and warning them against the schismatical Living Church. Furthermore, he called upon the hierarchs 'to administer their eparchies independently' [49] and only in dubious cases to turn to him for advice or adjudication. In this, Agathangel only followed the earlier directives of Tikhon.

At the same time, the Patriarchal Synod sent out instructions forbidding any member of the Church to attend the forthcoming Sobor of the Living Church, branding it as spurious. For canonically a Sobor could be called only by the Patriarch or his *locum tenens*. It further ruled that the parishes whose clergy went over to the revolting body should not communicate with them in prayer, and if possible should dismiss them. Furthermore, such parishes should immediately seek another priest from the local bishop, and if he too should have joined the Living Church, from the neighboring bishop faithful to the Patriarch. Thus the parishes were authorized to act in self-defense.

The 'purge' of the hierarchy conducted by the Living Church was in accordance with the program adopted by the party at an All-Russian Conference held in Moscow early in August. At that time they decided not only to deprive the patriarchal party of episcopal leadership, but to divest the parishes of their right to choose their priests. Nevertheless, the decision was not taken without vigorous dissension within the ranks of the Living Church. Dr. Julius Hecker — at that time friendly to the 'liberals' — reported that 'of the ninety-seven diocesan bishops, thirty-seven accepted the Living Church platform, thirty-six were against it, and twenty-four were undecided.' [50] According to Tikhon, eighty bishops of his party were deposed. The ruthless action of the new masters of the Russian Church forced the waverers to choose one way or another. The places of the dispossessed were promptly filled with the 'reformist' bishops. Even some 'loyal' hierarchs, members of the patriarchal Holy Synod, accepted the new administration. Among them were Metropolitan Sergei of Vladimir, later Tikhon's successor in the patriarchate, Archbishops Evdokim of Nizhni Novgorod (Gorki) and Seraphim of Kostroma, and Bishop Tikhon of Voronezh.[51]

Lay leadership in parishes showed itself resolutely opposed to the schismatic movement within the Church, and remained by and large faithful to the patriarchal party. They refused to accept the new diocesan administration and sometimes even drove the Living Church priests out of parishes. The patriarchal clergy, on the other hand, were vigorously supported by the lay element and extended their ministration beyond the limits of their own parishes. Hence, their parishes grew in numbers and their churches were thronged with worshipers, while their competitors were steadily losing lay support.

This obvious trend in support of the patriarchal party caused the Living Church to disintegrate into a number of smaller groups, although the Living Church remained the largest among them: the others were the Union of Ancient

Apostolic Churches, led by Vvedensky, and the Renovated Church, headed by Bishop Antonin.

After a year of such preparations, the 'reformists' felt secure enough in their strength to convene what they called the Second All-Russian Sobor. It was held in the beautiful Cathedral of Christ the Saviour in Moscow, and opened its sessions on 29 April 1923. Among the 430 voting delegates (of whom 308 were clerics, 122 were laymen), the Living Church had the absolute majority (250). The patriarchal party was represented by only fifteen 'old' bishops and thirty other delegates. These had been elected by their archdioceses or parishes despite the order of the Patriarchal Holy Synod forbidding co-operation with the Sobor. Among the few guests was Bishop Edgar Blake, unofficially representing the Methodist Episcopal Church of the United States. On 3 May Alexander Vvedensky delivered a speech in which he denounced the patriarchal form of ecclesiastical administration, particularly singling out Tikhon for his excoriation. He declared him an active enemy of the Soviet government. Krasnitsky, the leader of the Living Church party, supported him in these denunciations.

The first resolution expressed the Sobor's 'gratitude to the All-Russian Central Executive Committee' for permission to convene, and affirmed 'that every honorable Christian should take his place among these warriors for humanitarian truth (i.e. communists) and use all means to realize in life the grand principles of the October Revolution.' [52]

In its resolutions, the Sobor further declared that

The Soviet power does not appear as a persecutor of the Church. The Constitution of the Soviet state provides full religious liberty. . . . The freedom of religious propaganda (on a par with the progaganda of anti-religious ideas) gives the believers

opportunity to defend the values of their purely religious con-
victions. Therefore, Church people must not see in the Soviet
state a power of the anti-Christ; on the contrary, the Sobor
calls attention to the fact that the Soviet power is the only
one which attempts by state methods to realize the ideals of
the Kingdom of God.

The Council further condemned the Karlovtsi Sobor
for its various anti-Soviet acts and excommunicated all its
members. Furthermore, in its later sessions, the Sobor declared capitalism to be the 'great lie' and a 'mortal sin';
recognized the Soviet government as 'the world leader toward fraternity, equality, and international peace'; declared members of the 'white' parochial clergy — even
married ones — eligible for the episcopal office; approved
such married priests as had already been elevated to the
episcopal rank; permitted a second marriage to priests, but
not to bishops; and adopted the Gregorian calendar.

Consecration of the 'white' clergy to the episcopal office
even preceded the decision of the Sobor. In 1922, two
bishops, former priests, had been thus consecrated, and
other such acts followed. In accordance with this revolutionary legislation — uncanonical, since no particular
church could change the canons, that being the prerogative
of a General Council — Archpriest Alexander Vvedensky
was elevated to the post of the Archbishop of Krutitse.

But the central stage of the Sobor was occupied by the
trial and condemnation of Patriarch Tikhon. This farce
resulted in his adjudication — *in absentia* — first by the
episcopal Council under the presidency of Bishop Antonin,
which unanimously declared him deprived 'of his clerical
orders and of his patriarchal office.' [53] Thereupon, the whole
Sobor passed a similar judgment on him for his 'counter-
revolutionary activity.' It further declared Tikhon's anath-

ema pronounced upon the Soviet government in 1918 annulled, and deprived him not only of his clerical orders, but added to the episcopal verdict deprivation of his 'monastic vows and relegated him to his original lay status.' [54] Thereupon, the Sobor abolished the patriarchate altogether and changed the title of the Supreme Ecclesiastical Administration into the Supreme Church Council, declaring it to be the governing body of the Church. The new body was composed of representatives of all three factions: the Living Church received ten seats on it, the Union of the Ancient Apostolic Churches six, and the Renovated Church two. Despite that, however, Antonin was elevated to the post of 'Metropolitan of Moscow and all Russia.' As Stratonov ironically asks, what is the difference between 'Metropolitan of all Russia' and Patriarch? [55]

Before adjourning, the Sobor issued the customary address to the faithful in which it frankly admitted that it was 'forced to . . . adopt revolutionary measures for renewing the Church on the basis of gospel principles and apostolic traditions.' [56] It sought to justify its 'revolutionary measures' by citing the recognition accorded it by a number of 'patriarchal' hierarchs:

A large number of our best hierarchs, such as Metropolitan Sergei of Vladimir, Archbishop Evdokim of Nizhni Novgorod, and many other hierarchs of our church hastened to confirm by their acknowledgement the complete canonicity and legality of the Supreme Church Administration, and now in every way cooperate in its difficult task with the party of the white Orthodox clergy, the Living Church.[57]

III

It seemed at the time that the victory of the revolutionary movement within the Church was complete. The trial of

Tikhon before the Moscow Tribunal, for which the admission tickets had already been distributed, was expected to result in the verdict of death. This was regarded as beyond all doubt. But during his imprisonment the government approached him with the suggestion that resulted in a surprising and wholly unexpected *volte-face* in the Soviet official policy, so amazing to the outsiders. On 25 June the Court ruled that Tikhon be released, and the next day he was free. Two days later, the *Izvestiya* published the so-called *Confession* of Tikhon which explained the surprising event. In this document, the Patriarch admitted that

Having been nurtured in a monarchist society, and until my arrest having been under the influence of anti-Soviet individuals, I was filled with hostility against the Soviet authorities. . . . Acknowledging the correctness of the accusations of the Supreme Court and its sentence as conforming to the clauses of the criminal code, I repent of all my actions directed against the government and petition the Supreme Court to change its sentence and to set me free.

I declare hereby to the Soviet authorities that henceforth I am no more an enemy to the Soviet government and that I have completely and resolutely severed all connections with the foreign and domestic monarchists and the counter-revolutionary activity of the White Guards.[58]

There existed, naturally enough, a great deal of skepticism, or at least of speculation, whether the text of this declaration had not been dictated to the Patriarch by the authorities. In an interview published in the *Manchester Guardian*, Tikhon declared:

I have never sought to overthrow the government. In 1918, I stood openly against some of its decrees. I am not a counter-revolutionary, in spite of the fact that some of my appeals had an anti-Soviet character. The power of the Soviet government has greatly increased in Russia; and it has undergone various

developments. We, the members of the old clergy, are not now struggling against the Soviets, but against the Living Church. What were the causes of your liberation and the change in the attitude of the Soviet government toward you?
I am persuaded that, having studied my case, the government has convinced itself that I am no counter-revolutionary. It was suggested that I should make a public declaration of the fact, and I wrote a letter to say so.[59]

The trouble with this statement is that in the 'Confession' he admits that he had been a counter-revolutionary, while in the interview he denies it. When he asserts that he had 'completely and resolutely severed all connections with the foreign and domestic monarchists,' that is of course true ever since 1918; why had not the government believed him? One also wonders what form the 'suggestion' of the government that he 'make a public declaration' took.

Upon his release, at the first liturgy which he celebrated at the Donskoy monastery, Tikhon spoke to an immense crowd which came to greet him. He urged them to throw aside all political opposition to the regime, and to stand loyally by the Church. To his intimates he revealed his intention to work for the attainment of a *'modus vivendi'* with the government. Upon securing it, he intended to call a new Sobor from which he would seek an approval of his conduct of affairs.[60] He then sent a letter 'To the Archpastors, Pastors, and Members of the Orthodox Church' (28 June) branding the claims of the Supreme Church Council as 'lies and fraud,' and its powers as illegal. He consequently pronounced the Sobor of 1923 uncanonical, its decisions invalid, and its leaders and adherents excommunicated.[61] He furthermore declared 'all arrangements made during our absence by those ruling the Church, since they had neither the legal right nor canonical authority, are non-valid and void, and all actions and sacraments performed by bishops and clergymen who have forsaken the Church are devoid of God's grace and power.' He further announced that he once again assumed 'the primate's authority which we had temporarily transferred to our substitute, Metropolitan Agathangel.' [62]

In this struggle with the schismatics Tikhon proved victorious, because the vast masses of the lay members of the Church remained faithful to him. It was this circumstance that moved the governmental authorities to abandon the adherents of the Supreme Church Council and other 'synodical' groups who had hitherto been favored and supported by them. The Living Church leaders held a Conference in August 1923, which once again reorganized the structure of that body and voted to suspend 'temporarily' the radical measures adopted by the Sobor. But they refused by and large to accept the demand of the Patriarch that they return to his obedience by way of penance and submission. Three members of the Patriarchal Synod entered into negotiations with them, but after a time dropped these *pourparlers* as fruitless. Nevertheless, many leaders of the schismatic groups returned to Tikhon's obedience — among them even Protopriest V. Krasnitsky, who was restored and admitted as a member of the Patriarchal Council. But Metropolitan Evdokim and the married Archbishop Vvedensky refused to capitulate. They endeavored to damage Tikhon's reputation both with the rank and file of the faithful and with the government: they called him 'an adventurer,' and a 'sectarian schismatic,' and claimed that the Ecumenical Patriarch, Gregory VII, had recognized them rather than Tikhon as the lawful administrators of the Church. This latter statement was actually true: for Gregory, having been appealed to by the Russian synodical leaders to render judgment in the dispute between them and the Patriarch, appointed a commission to investigate the affair. He instructed the commission to recognize as legal the party loyal to the Soviet government, but practically prejudged the investigation by advising Tikhon to resign 'for the sake of uniting the Church and for the sake of his flock.' [63] Naturally, Tikhon refused to accept the 'advice' and reminded his fellow-patriarch that it is against the canons for a foreign prelate 'to intrude himself into the life and affairs of the autocephalous Russian Church,' particularly as it was done 'without any preparatory correspondence with us as the lawful representative and head' of that Church.

Patriarch Tikhon had twice issued directives as to who was to act as his *locum tenens* in case of his death and before his successor could be elected; the first of these documents was issued shortly after his release from prison in 1923. But in January 1925 he changed the instructions by appointing to that post Metropolitans Kirill, Agathangel, and Peter of Krutitse. They were to assume office in the order given.

The need for such directives appeared in December 1924: he had fallen ill, and according to Stratonov's account,[64] in January was taken to the hospital kept by the Bakunins in Ostrozhenka. He was ordered by the doctors to relinquish all work. For the first two weeks, Tikhon's recovery progressed fairly well. He read a great deal, particularly the Russian classics. But he did not entirely give up his official duties. He also received many visits, particularly of Metropolitan Peter, who was in charge of the Moscow archdiocese.

Having greatly improved in health, Tikhon began to celebrate the liturgy on Sundays and holidays, and to attend more and more to his official duties. The doctors protested, but the Patriarch resolutely insisted that he must not neglect his work. Finally, he resumed his attendance at the sessions of the Holy Synod. Protests availed nothing. Consequently, his health took a turn for the worse. Moreover, he suffered with toothache which did not allow him to sleep without a morphine injection. When the teeth were extracted, he was greatly weakened. The doctors thereupon forbade him to leave the hospital. But Tikhon disobeyed them. On 25 March/7 April, toward the evening, he insisted that important business necessitated his presence at the session of the Synod. He returned at 10 o'clock, very tired. His condition greatly alarmed the hospital staff: they called Tikhon's physician, who quieted the patient by administering morphine. The physician left at about 11 p.m.; within an hour the Patriarch suffered his fourth and final attack of *angina pectoris*. The hospital doctor declared him dead.

The news of Tikhon's death spread throughout Moscow the same night, and by 7 a.m. Ostrozhenka was thronged with a dense crowd of people. His body was taken to the Donskoy monastery and placed on display. The funeral was held five days later. 'Moscow never beheld such a mass of people as had gathered for the funeral.' The services lasted from ten in the morning till six in the afternoon, and the entire gathering remained to the end.

Stratonov's detailed and circumstantial description of the Patriarch's illness and death is squarely contradicted in several important details by a member of the Karlovtsi group, M. Polsky.[65] He asserts that during Tikhon's last illness it was found necessary to remove him to a nursing home kept by a woman-physician, Dr. Bakunina, whose husband was a surgeon. Either both of the Bakunins or she alone escaped to France, where she was in charge of the Russian House at Sainte-Geneviève des Bois, an old people's home. She testified that on the day of Tikhon's death, Metropolitan Peter of Krutitse had been with the Patriarch for some hours prior to his demise. The conversation between the two hierarchs was loud and stormy, so that she debated. with herself about whether or not she should interfere. Then about two hours before Tikhon died, Peter had emerged from the room carrying a paper in his hand. It is inferred that this was the 'Will,' and that it was Peter who had persuaded Tikhon to sign the document. Even if this story is true, there is no proof that it was the 'Will' — although that document was signed on the day that Tikhon died.[66]

In this crucially important document, the authenticity of which is not questioned, the Patriarch called upon the faithful to render steadfast loyalty to the Soviet government:

Without sinning against our faith or Church, without surrendering anything of them, in a word, without permitting any compromises or concessions in the realm of belief, in our relation as citizens we must be sincere in our attitude toward the Soviet government . . . condemning all association with the enemies of the Soviet government and all open or secret agitation against it.

. . . We call upon the parochial societies, and especially upon their executive officials, not to admit any individuals of antigovernmental inclinations, nor to nurture hopes for the restoration of the monarchical system, but to become convinced that the Soviet government is actually the government of workers and peasants, and hence durable and stable.

. . . In deference to the duty incumbent upon us to guard the purity of Church life . . . we cannot but condemn those who, in forgetfulness of the divine ends, misuse their ecclesiastical position by giving themselves beyond measure to the human, and often degraded, political game, sometimes even of a culpable character; therefore, in accordance with the duty of our office as primate, we approve of appointing a special commission to be charged with the investigation, and if declared proper, even removal from office, in accordance with the canonical rules, of those hierarchs and priests who persist in their perversity and refuse to repent of it before the Soviet government, and to bring such before the tribunal of the Orthodox Sobor.

At the same time, we must mention with deep sorrow that certain sons of Russia, and even hierarchs and priests, have left the fatherland for various reasons, and have already busied themselves in activities to which they have not been called and which in any case are injurious to our Church. Making use of our name and our ecclesiastical authority, they have carried on harmful and counter-revolutionary activity. We positively declare that we have no connection with them, as our enemies affirm; they are strangers to us, and we condemn their harmful activity. . . . The so-called Sobor of Karlovtsi brought no blessing to the Church or the nation, and we again confirm its condemnation, and hold it necessary to proclaim firmly and positively that any such further attempt will call forth on our part extreme measures, even to the forbidding of the ministry and trial by the tribunal of the Sobor. In order to avoid such severe penalties, we call upon all hierarchs and priests abroad to cease from their political activity in connection with the enemies of our nation, and to have the manliness to return to the fatherland and to speak the truth about themselves and the Church of God.

. . . We order that a special commission investigate the activity of the hierarchs and priests who have fled abroad, and especially of Metropolitan Antony, formerly of Kiev; Platon, formerly of Odessa; as well as others, and immediately to prepare a statement concerning their activity. Their refusal to submit to our demand will oblige us to judge them *in absentia*.

Our enemies . . . are spreading lying rumors that we are not at liberty in our patriarchal office to speak freely, and even are not free in conscience; . . . We declare all such inventions regarding our lack of freedom to be lies and seduction, for there is no government on earth which could bind our sacerdotal conscience or our patriarchal word. . . .

As has been indicated, the circumstances under which the declaration was made are in question, particularly as regards the date of its composition. Furthermore, there are two glaring inconsistencies in it — which, however, are easily explainable, if we assume that the document was signed just before Tikhon's death. The Patriarch asserts therein that 'Now we, by the grace of God, having regained our health, again entering upon the service of the Church of God . . .' This sentence is in obvious contradiction to the fact. The difficulty is removed, however, when we realize that the Patriarch was not only unaware of the approaching end, but actually regarded himself as having recovered from his illness. The same applies to the dating of the document, given as 'Donskoy Monastery, April 7, 1925.' This yields the additional insight into his intention of actually returning that very day to his official residence; he dated the paper thus in anticipation of the removal.

IV

When, in the summer of 1926, I stood — quite alone — before the grave of Patriarch Tikhon in the Donskoy monastery, I tried to formulate an opinion of him on the basis of the facts I had then collected. The members of the synodical party, I knew, still regarded him as a jolly but weak and easily dominated sort of man.[67] His popularity was attested by all, whether enemies or friends. Comrade P. D. Smidovich, in charge of ecclesiastical affairs, whom I had interviewed before that time, had expressed the same judgment about Tikhon: personally a good man, but weak and lacking in will power; hence, easily influenced by those who surrounded him.

Having had an opportunity to reflect upon these estimates of Tikhon's character in the light of whatever further information I could get during the almost thirty years which have elapsed since, I see reasons for modifying this judgment. The policy of opposition to the Soviet government adhered to during Tikhon's first year in the patriarchal office could lead only to defeat — as it actually did. Had Antony Khrapovitsky been elected Patriarch, and had he actually persisted in his monarchical and anti-Soviet policy come what may, such a course would have been suicidal for the Church. For it would have played directly into the hands of the regime which aimed at the *ultimate* destruction of the Church. The Church, after all, is above politics, and must not make itself into a last ditch stronghold of any political system. Hence, Tikhon wisely changed his policies, particularly when he saw, from his house and the GPU prison windows, that the Church had fallen prey to the schismatics who had gained the favor of the government by their loud professions of civil loyalty. Tikhon therefore early adopted the policy of non-interference in politics, hoping to secure, in strict conformity with the legal and constitutional separation of Church and state, full autonomy of the former. Thus he hoped to secure for his patriarchal party not only a victory over the schism, but the eventual legitimation of the status of the Russian Orthodox Church in the Soviet Union. But he did not become subservient to the state as his successors were either forced, or voluntarily chose, to be.

Hence there appears no clear reason for charging him with weakness or lack of will power. His moderation and willingness to change his policy testify to good sense and administrative ability, such as his chief opponent, the head-strong and obstinate Metropolitan Antony, or his 'synodical' rivals, did not possess. Patriarch Tikhon was a wise, moderate, and responsible leader of the Russian Orthodox Church, whose lot fell upon unusually difficult times.

In the words of the memorial oration delivered by the Russian theologian Sergei Bulgakov, in Prague (which words now essentially express my estimate of Tikhon's policy and aims):

[the Patriarch] in his relations with the State, which under the mask of separation of Church and State was openly hostile to the Church, . . . worked for the preservation of the Church's independence. Under the existing conditions, when all possibility of normal interaction between Church and State was excluded — this independence could be realized only by complete aloofness of the Church from the State; in other words, by the Church being non-political and thus indeed separate from the State. Though this state of things was far from being desirable under the conditions, it answered best to the dignity of the Church. The Patriarch preserved the Church from identification with the White movement — inasmuch as that movement was not an expression of the mind of the majority of the people, which had not yet passed out of the disease of Bolshevism. He preserved the Church from any too much connection with any of the political groups, as became apparent after the Karlovitz Synod of the *émigré* churches. He preserved the Church from being swallowed up by the sinister element of the 'Living Church,' which aimed at making it an obedient tool of the Soviet government . . . The 'Living Church' had come to life in the quarters of the political police, and from thence found constant support . . . In open fight with the Church, the 'Living Church' was defeated, and the Patriarch emerged victorious, though a prisoner, but strong in the faith and trust of the people.[68]

NOTES

¹ A. P. Rozhdestvensky, *Svateishy Tikhon, patriarkh Moskovsky i vseya Rossii* (Sofia, Bulgaria, n.d.), 5. My biographical sketch of Tikhon is largely based on this memoir written by the life-long friend of the patriarch.

² Ibid. 6–7.

³ Sergius Bulgakov, *The Orthodox Church* (London, 1935), 48ff.

⁴ Metropolitan Evlogy, *Put' moei zhizni* (Paris, Y.M.C.A. Press, 1947), 93.

⁵ John S. Curtiss, *The Russian Church and the Soviet State, 1917–1950* (Boston, 1953), 10–12.

⁶ A. Vvedensky, *Tserkov i gosudarstvo* (Moscow, 1923), 32.

⁷ Prince Gregory Trubetskoy, *Krasnaya Rossiya i svyataya Rus* (Paris, 1931), 41.

⁸ Ibid. 42.

⁹ Quoted in Curtiss, op. cit. 31.

¹⁰ Trubetskoy, op. cit. 43.

¹¹ This account is based on the description of an eye-witness, Metropolitan Evlogy, in his *Put' moei zhizni*, 299–335; also cf. Matthew Spinka, *The Church and the Russian Revolution* (New York, 1927), 81–91.

¹² Trubetskoy, op. cit. 43.

¹³ Vvedensky, op. cit. 110.

¹⁴ N. Bukharin, *Tserkov i shkola* (Moscow, 1918), 3.

¹⁵ Frank A. Golder, *Documents of Russian History: 1914–1917* (New York, 1927), 623. Reprinted by permission of Appleton-Century-Crofts, Inc.

¹⁶ The entire text is to be found in Spinka, op. cit. 118–22.

¹⁷ David Shub, *Lenin* (Doubleday & Company, New York, 1950), 146–52.

¹⁸ S. V. Troitsky, *Chto sdyelal Patriarkh Tikhon dlya tserkvi i rodiny* (Odessa, 1919), 11–12.

¹⁹ The text is found in Spinka, op. cit. 104–6.

²⁰ Julius Hecker, *Religion under the Soviets* (New York, 1927), 66.

²¹ Ibid. 70, footnote.

²² Troitsky, op. cit. 13; also Trubetskoy, op. cit. 145–6.

²³ V. Gidulyanov, *Otdeleniye tserkvi ot gosudarstva v SSSR* (Moscow, 1926), 29.

²⁴ Rozhdestvensky, op. cit. 19.

²⁵ Troitsky, *Chto sdyelal Patriarkh Tikhon dlya tserkvi*, 14; Curtiss, op. cit. 64–5.

[26] Paul B. Anderson (ed.), *Life in Soviet Russia*, No. 10 (Paris, 1935), 40–43; for other details, see Trubetskoy, op. cit. 47; also Curtiss, op. cit. 87.

[27] G. Fedotov, *I est i budet* (Paris, 1932), 132f.

[28] I. Stratonov, *Russkaya tserkovnaya smuta, 1921–1931* (Berlin, 1932), 13.

[29] Ibid. 13–14.

[30] Ibid. 14.

[31] S. Troitsky, *Razmezhevanie ili Raskol* (Paris, 1932), 74; Curtiss, op. cit. 94.

[32] *Tserkovnya Vedomosti* No. 10 and 11, 1922, 2.

[33] This whole account follows Stratonov, op. cit. 26–31.

[34] Ibid. 31.

[35] Ibid. 32–4; Curtiss, op. cit. 113–44.

[36] Ibid. 37; also Metropolitan Evlogy, op. cit. 402–3.

[37] Spinka, op. cit. 173.

[38] Ibid. 176.

[39] Curtiss, op. cit. 63.

[40] Stratonov, op. cit. 43.

[41] The account of the trial is found in *Chernaya Kniga* (Paris, 1925), 198–238.

[42] Stratonov, op. cit. 48.

[43] Other examples are given in W. C. Emhardt, *Religion in Soviet Russia* (Milwaukee, Morehouse-Gorham, 1929), 48ff.

[44] Stratonov, op. cit. 50; also Spinka, op. cit. 197.

[45] Spinka, op. cit. 190ff.

[46] Stratonov, op. cit. 164.

[47] *Izvestiya*, 16 April 1922; Spinka, op. cit. 257; Stratonov, op. cit. 52.

[48] Stratonov, op. cit. 54.

[49] Ibid. 55.

[50] Hecker, op. cit. 89.

[51] B. V. Titlinov, *Novaya tserkov* (Moscow, 1923), 20.

[52] Spinka, op. cit. 237.

[53] Ibid., 240.

[54] Ibid. 242.

[55] Stratonov, op. cit. 77.

[56] Emhardt, op. cit. 66.

[57] Ibid.

[58] See the full text in Spinka, op. cit. 250–57; Curtiss, op. cit. 159–60.

[59] See the full text in Spinka, op. cit. 253–4.

[60] Emhardt, op. cit. 134.

[61] See the full text in Spinka, op. cit. 255–60.

[62] Ibid. 258–9.

[63] Spinka, op. cit. 276; also Stratonov, op. cit. 100.

[64] Stratonov, op. cit. 124–7.

[65] M. Polsky, *Kanonicheskoe polozhenie vysshei tserkovnoi vlasti v SSSR i zagranitsei* (Jordanville, N. Y., Holy Trinity Monastery, 1948), 24.

[66] The full text of the 'Will' is in Spinka, op. cit. 285–9.

[67] Hecker, op. cit. 115.

[68] *The Slavonic Review* (London, June 1925), IV, No. 10, pp. 162–3.

II

PATRIARCH SERGEI

CAPITULATES TO SAVE THE CHURCH

THE historic moment of the modern Russian Orthodox Church occurred in 1927 when Metropolitan
Sergei, then the acting 'Guardian of the Patriarchal
Throne,' succeeded in 'registering' himself and his temporary Holy Synod with the government as the recognized
administrator of the Church. He thus terminated the
period during which the hierarchy had been practically
outlawed. Since according to the Law of Separation of
1918 only local congregations were officially recognized
entities, the Patriarch or his successors, along with all
bishops and metropolitans belonging to the patriarchal
party, were not recognized as the administrators of the
Church. The anti-patriarchal parties, on the other hand,
enjoyed governmental favor and their leaders exercised
centralized administration. Sergei's act of 'registration'
secured for him and his temporary Holy Synod governmental recognition of his canonical powers, and thus restored to him the administrative functions belonging to
his office. Hence, the eighteen years of his term of office
proved of epochal significance for the Russian Orthodox
Church and for the shaping of the Soviet ecclesiastical
policies.

I

Sergei was born on 11 January 1867, in Arzamas, near Nizhni Novgorod, of a priestly family. His father, Proto-priest Nikolai Ivanovich Stragorodsky, was serving in the Arzamas-Alexeievsky convent. The boy received in baptism the name of Ivan Nikolaievich. His mother died soon after his birth. He began his education in the parish school, from which he passed to the local church schools, and later to the archdiocesan priestly seminary in Nizhni Novgorod. He graduated in 1886, but instead of entering upon the clerical career, he decided to continue his studies in the St. Petersburg Theological Academy. In this institution of higher theological studies (comparable to our graduate theological seminaries) he chose to major in history and minor in languages. Proving himself a diligent and able student, he graduated with distinction, receiving his master's degree after five years of study. His thesis, declared by his professors to be a scholarly piece of work, dealt with the subject, 'The Orthodox Doctrine of Salvation.'

Thereupon, if he so wished, he could have chosen an academic career as his life work; but instead, he decided to assume the monastic habit — the prerequisite for the episcopal or other administrative offices. On 30 January 1890, Ivan Nikolaievich Stragorodsky became the monk Sergei, and thus took the initial step in a career which led him to the patriarchal throne. At his own request, he was appointed a member of the Russian Orthodox mission to Japan, where he arrived in October of that year. But he did not remain there long: after three years he was recalled to St. Petersburg and appointed a docent of Old Testament studies in the Theological Academy. For some reason he held this academic post only a few months, having been transferred then to the office of Inspector of the Moscow Theological Academy located at Zagorsk in the historic Trinity-Sergei monastery about thirty miles north of Moscow. A year later, already holding the rank of archimandrite, Sergei was once more transferred, this time to Athens, where he was placed in charge of the Russian Embassy church. These rapid and somewhat bewildering changes were necessitated, we are told, by the state of his health. He found the Russian climate too severe; hence the transfer to Athens.

Between 1897 and 1899 he again served the Japanese Orthodox mission, but in the latter year was appointed rector of the St. Petersburg Theological Seminary, and two years later he became rector of his alma mater, the St. Petersburg Theological Academy. At the same time, he was elevated to the episcopal rank with the title of Bishop of Yamburg (the third vicar of the St. Petersburg archdiocese). The consecration ceremony was performed by the Metropolitan of St. Petersburg, Antony (Vadkovsky), who was assisted by the metropolitans of Moscow and Kiev and other high Church dignitaries. During this phase of his career, Sergei gained an excellent reputation not only among the theological students, but even among the leading intellectuals (generally alienated from the Church). For he presided over the discussions held by the 'Religious-philosophical Meetings' and attended by both clergy and educated laity; among the latter were such distinguished writers and philosophers as Dmitry S. Merezhkovsky, V. V. Rozanov, and Nicholas Berdyaev. Berdyaev wrote about these discussions:

The meetings were remarkable in that they constituted the first confrontation of the leaders of Russian culture and literature, who were painfully aware of their religious disquietude, with the representatives of the traditional Orthodox Church hierarchy.[1]

It was during these years of Sergei's rectorship that he became acquainted with 'Grishka' Rasputin, and introduced him to Archimandrite Theophan — the father-confessor of the Grand Duchesses Militsa Nikolaevna and Anastasia Nikolaevna — who in turn brought him to the attention of the Tsar and Tsarina. The consequences, as is well known, were catastrophic. But it must be said that at that time Rasputin had not yet gained the notoriety which his dissolute life and his overweening influence at the Court later brought him.[2]

Sergei gained for himself a reputation for 'liberalism' when, during the stirring days of the First Russian Revolution (1905), he courageously defended the tsar's grant of religious toleration to the Orthodox and non-Orthodox nonconformists. He even advocated such a radical measure as the separation of Church and state which far exceeded the modest reforms contemplated by the government. Testimony to his liberal tendencies is likewise borne by the rector of the Kholm Seminary, Evlogy, who visited Sergei in Petersburg at this time and found the company the latter kept somewhat too liberal.[3]

Sergei's rapid promotion in his ecclesiastical career was greatly furthered when in 1905 he was elevated to the archiepiscopal rank and assigned the archdiocese of Finland and Vyborg. Six years later he received the signal honor of being appointed a member of the Holy Governing Synod, in which capacity he was made chairman of two important committees — the educational and the missionary. Moreover, it was perhaps for that reason that Sergei was further honored by being chosen to preside over the summer session of the Synod.[4] Thus at the comparatively youthful age of forty-four, he already occupied an important place in the highest administrative body of the Russian Orthodox Church.

The official biography (upon which I cautiously draw, although well knowing that it systematically omits anything which might be regarded as derogatory to Sergei) makes no mention of the incident narrated by a member of the *émigré* clergy strongly opposed to the 'Sergeian Church,' but I decided to include it for what it may be worth despite the fact that no other source attests the story. This source alleges that when Rasputin, relying on the support of the tsar and the tsarina, attempted to force upon the Holy Synod the appointment of Varvara, an unworthy candidate for the episcopal office, the president of the Synod, Metropolitan Antony of St. Petersburg, refused to yield to the pressure brought upon him from the highest quarters. However, during the Metropolitan's absence, Archbishop Sergei, presiding over the Synod, 'put the measure through.'[5] The story admittedly does not ring true; for when the Ober-Procurator Lvov in 1917 decided to rid the Holy Governing Synod of reactionaries, he expelled the known Rasputinites and did not include Sergei among them. In fact, Sergei was reappointed to membership in the new Synod. But it is more reliably established that when the Duma denounced Rasputin's influence in the Synod, particularly in the case of the Ober-Procurator V. K. Sabler, Sergei energetically and demonstratively defended the latter.[6] One cannot help wondering whether it was as a reward for such services that the government decorated Sergei with the order of St. Alexander Nevsky.

When the First World War broke out in 1914, it soon engulfed most of the major nations of the world and caused gigantic, world-wide changes in the political and economic spheres. In Russia itself — as has already been mentioned — the catastrophic events unleashed by the war brought about the downfall of the tsarist regime, with the consequent radical reconstruction of the ecclesiastical structure of the Russian Church.

When the Synod was reorganized by the new Ober-Procurator, V. N. Lvov, Sergei and Platon were the only members of the former body to be reappointed.[7] In fact, Sergei was placed at the head of the new Synod.[8] This indicates, perhaps better than anything else, that he was regarded, even by the relatively liberal elements of the population represented in the Provisional Government, as favorably inclined toward the current political order of things. He was at the time chosen Archbishop of Vladimir.

When Metropolitan Tikhon was elected Patriarch, he promptly organized the Holy Synod, and Sergei, who was raised in November to the rank of Metropolitan, became one of its members, although not the first in rank. He was arrested and imprisoned by the Bolsheviks after they seized power in November 1917, although he was released shortly after.[9]

In January 1918, as has already been related, the Soviet regime promulgated its first ecclesiastical legislation, whereby it decreed the separation of the Church from the state and the school from the Church.[10] Patriarch Tikhon promptly protested against this legislation as discriminatory and unjust, excommunicated its authors, and forbade the clergy and the faithful to observe its provisions. This action inaugurated a struggle between the Church and the state the outcome of which, in case the Bolsheviks succeeded in retaining political power, could not have been in doubt. When in 1922 the Patriarch was imprisoned, and a group of clergy in revolt seized the supreme power in the Church, Metropolitan Sergei of Vladimir and Archbishops Evdokim of Nizhni Novgorod, Seraphim of Kostroma, Tikhon of Voronezh, and many others, gave their approval to the new body as 'having been called forth by canonical necessity.' [11] Professor Titlinov, one of the best-known publicists of the Living Church, wrote that the above-named hierarchs 'co-operate in every way in its [Supreme Administration's] difficult task, as well as with the party of the "white" Orthodox clergy, "The Living Church." ' [12] It was even asserted that Sergei was offered the chairman-ship of the Synod of the Living Church, but declined. At any rate, as soon as Patriarch Tikhon was released from prison, Sergei whole-heartedly returned to his obedience. Thereafter, Titlinov himself testified that Sergei 'has shown himself to be one of the most irreconcilable' oppo-nents of the Living Church.[13]

When Patriarch Tikhon was released from prison, Metro-politan Sergei (January 1924) made a public confession of his error:

Publicly, on his knees before the Patriarch, dressed in the garb of a simple monk, he made an act of penitence, and after this received anew from the Patriarch the 'mitra' (cowl) of a metro-politan.[14]

He was thereupon reinstated as a member of the patriarchal Holy Synod.[15] To show how history is written in the Soviet Union, even under the patriarchal auspices, I shall quote the exquisite understatement regarding Patriarch Tikhon which covers this whole period from 1917 to 1925 in the following inimitable sentence: 'In the year 1923 the Most Holy Patriarch again received the possibility factually to administer the Church, but did not succeed in restoring peace to the Church; for he died on March 25 [old style].' [16]

At the time of Tikhon's death, only Metropolitan Peter of all those appointed to serve in such capacity, was at liberty to take over the duties of 'the Guardian of the Patriarchal Throne.' Kirill had been sent into exile, and Agathangel had not been allowed to come to Moscow. Peter (Polyansky) had been for many years prior to the Revolution a member of the Educational Committee of the Holy Governing Synod. In 1917 he assumed the monastic habit, and Patriarch Tikhon made him his vicar with the title of the Bishop of Podolsk. When Archbishop Ilarion of Krutitse, the administrator of the Moscow archdiocese, was arrested, Tikhon transferred Peter to that influential and responsible post.[17] It was while holding this office that Peter assumed the direction of Church affairs after Tikhon's death. But if he had hoped that Tikhon's 'Will' would ameliorate the government's attitude toward the patriarchal Church, he was mistaken. For despite the reiterated profession of Tikhon's and the Church's loyalty to the regime, the policy of persecution of the Church was not stopped. Metropolitan Peter himself, having resolutely refused the overtures of the schismatics to acknowledge the canonicity of their Sobor of 1923 was denounced for alleged disloyalty.[18] Vvedensky claimed to possess a document purporting to prove the connection of Peter with the counter-revolutionaries abroad, and particularly with the Grand Duke Kirill Vladimirovich, a claimant of the Russian throne. Stratonov writes:

There can be no doubt that the document was a forgery. What gave color to this charge was the fact that the representative of the Restorationist Synod, Bishop Nikolai Solovey, arriving abroad, returned to the patriarchal obedience, but at the same time wrote a letter to Kirill. This was utilized by the government and Vvedensky against Peter . . .[19]

Bishop Gregory of Ekaterinburg demanded that Peter publicly deny the charges, in order to prevent the involvement
of others in Peter's fate. He also suggested that a Council of
bishops try Peter and pass judgment on the allegations.[20]
But Peter refused these suggestions. Thereupon, Gregory
withdrew from Peter's obedience and organized a new
Supreme Church Council, composed of himself and six
hierarchs. Peter himself was arrested on 10 December 1925,
placed on trial, sentenced, and exiled, at first to the Island
of Khe at the mouth of the River Ob, and in September
1928 was transferred to Tobolsk. I myself called, on 18
August 1926, on Comrade P. D. Smidovich, one of the 'Five'
in charge of ecclesiastical affairs, and inquired what the
charges against Peter were. He replied that the GPU had
collected 'proofs' of Peter's complicity in the political
machinations of the monarchist groups abroad, and that he
had confessed to having sent his blessings to the Grand
Duke. Smidovich further asserted that Peter had already
signed the confession and begged for mercy. When I asked
to see a transcript of the court proceedings, he replied that
it would be published in the papers in the near future. To
my knowledge, no such report has ever made its appearance.[21] Later Peter was offered freedom, if he would approve Sergei's 'Declaration' of 1927, of which we shall speak
in due course. But he refused. Thereupon, his term of exile
was augmented by an additional three years. He died in
exile (1936), refusing to the end to acknowledge Sergei's
act.

II

With the exile of Metropolitan Peter, the administration
of the Church had to be reorganized again. Peter had taken

the wise precaution (6 December 1925) of appointing substitutes or deputies for himself in case he should be prevented from exercising the duties of his office. He had
chosen as temporary substitutes Metropolitan Mikhail of
the Ukraine, Metropolitan Joseph of Rostov, and Metropolitan Sergei of Nizhni Novgorod.[22] Since the two first-
named hierarchs had been arrested and exiled, the responsibility of deputizing for Peter devolved upon Sergei. It was
not without difficulty, however, that he retained his post.
In the first place, he was opposed by the Gregorian group,
comprising then about ten hierarchs, which had broken with
Peter. These malcontents had the daring to 'depose' Peter
himself and therefore refused to recognize Sergei as Peter's
deputy. Moreover, they secured recognition of the government as the rightful administrators of the Church. Thus
while the schism between Sergei and Gregory lasted, there
existed two Supreme Church Administrations — one in
Nizhni Novgorod and one in Moscow. Fortunately, the
Gregorian Council soon disintegrated, most of its members
acknowledging Peter as the lawful *locum tenens* and Sergei
as his substitute.[23]

But early in 1926 Sergei was arrested and placed in a
Moscow prison. While he remained detained, many of the
Gregory group went over to him. A new complication
arose when Metropolitan Agathangel returned from exile,
for he now claimed precedence over Peter as the rightful
locum tenens, since he had been named by Tikhon to that
office ahead of Peter. Sergei, released from prison, wrote
to Agathangel and also met him in a personal interview:
the two hierarchs finally concluded to leave things as they
were until Peter should be either freed or condemned by a
civil court. Agathangel confirmed this arrangement when
he telegraphed to Sergei: 'Continue to administer the

Church. I will refrain from all contrary steps. I will observe the decision about mentioning Metropolitan Peter [in the liturgy], for I intend, for the sake of peace, to resign as *locum tenens.*' [24] This was dated 27 May 1926. Peter subsequently approved this arrangement, which was thus made with his authority. So Sergei at last emerged as the *de facto* leader of the Church and was acknowledged as such by the majority of the hierarchy. He not only retained this position (although later he was elevated from mere deputy of the Guardian to Guardian) for the next seventeen years, but in 1943 succeeded in converting it into that of Patriarch.

As deputy of the *locum tenens,* Sergei confronted a task which seemed well-nigh hopeless, for to all intents and purposes the government had been able to disorganize the administration of the patriarchal Church so thoroughly that he and the hierarchs of the patriarchal party could hardly exert any effective control over it. It must be borne in mind that according to the initial (1918) and subsequent legislation, the only legal ecclesiastical unit recognized by law was the local congregation, registered with the authorities in accordance with the prescribed regulations; episcopal administration had no legal validity. Thus, neither Sergei nor any of his episcopal confreres had any legal standing in the eyes of the government. On the other hand, the ecclesiastical administration of the various schismatic, pro-Soviet bodies (the Living Church, the Renovated Church, etc.) exercised such administrative functions freely and with the help of the 'Five' (Trotsky, Smidovich, Krasikov, archpriest Galkin, and Tuchkov) who controlled the secret Department for Church Affairs of the *Sovnarkom.*[25] In contrast to that, Sergei was arrested once more early in 1926, and many hierarchs of the patriarchal party were sent into exile: the *Black Book,* published in 1925, lists sixty-six of them.[26] It was, therefore, a matter literally of life and death for the patriarchal Church to secure governmental recognition, and therewith permission to set up its own centralized administration. This task, which involved not only the recognition of and the profession of loyalty to the Soviet regime — after all, that had already been done by Tikhon and Peter — but the acceptance of all the regime's demands for virtual submission, fell to the lot of Sergei.

Under these circumstances, Sergei sent, sometime before 10 June 1926, an appeal to the government requesting that his Church administration be 'registered,' i.e. legally recognized by the government. We do not have the text of these negotiations.[27] On 10 June Sergei sent a letter to 'the bishops, priests, and the faithful of the patriarchate of Moscow,' [28] in which he not only informed them of his negotiations with the government, but positively asserted that they had been successful. In return for the expected benefits, Sergei pledged, in behalf of the Church, to refrain from all anti-Soviet activity. 'We promise freely that to the degree to which it depends upon our authority, we will not henceforth permit the Church to find itself involved in any political adventure whatever . . .' Sergei further frankly states that contradictions exist between the believers and the communists. He does not 'promise reconciliation of that which is irreconcilable,' nor does he pretend to adjust or adapt the Church to communism or other 'modern exigencies,' nor to modify its doctrines or canons; rather he flatly asserts that 'we will remain in our religious point of view what we are, i.e. members of the traditional Church.' But in promising civil loyalty, Sergei insists that the hierarchy 'cannot enter into any special engagement to prove our loyalty' or accept responsibility for the political views of the clergy, whether at home or abroad. He refuses to accept any responsibility for, or 'duty of, watching over the political tendencies of our correligionists . . . The Soviet government disposes of much more adequate organs for that purpose, and possesses much more efficient means.' In other words, Sergei refuses to have the Church used as (spiritual) police. He cites as the strongest reason for this stand that the Revolution itself had freed the Church from all political involvements and we 'assuredly cannot surrender that advantage.' He admits that some of the *émigré* clergy have engaged in anti-Soviet political activity, but disclaims, in behalf of the Church, all connection with them and all responsibility for their acts. To inflict ecclesiastical punishments on them would be ineffective and would make matters worse, for it would constitute a proof in the eyes of the *émigré* clergy that the Church at home was forced by the regime to take such action against them. Sergei declares that they 'ought to be excluded from the ecclesiastical community of the Moscow patriarchate and ought to place themselves under the jurisdiction of the Orthodox Churches where they reside.' [29]

In a similar vein Sergei wrote to the Karlovtsi bishops (30 September/12 October 1926), when they asked him to mediate between themselves and Metropolitan Evlogy. He declined to serve as a judge, and specifically asserted that since there was no actual contact between the Moscow supreme administration and the churches abroad, there could be no supervision or governing of these churches by Moscow. Consequently he concludes that 'in non-Orthodox countries independent congregations or churches may be organized, members of which may be even non-Russians . . . Think it over, please. For such a solution of the problem obviously corresponds better to the existing circumstances even of our Church.' [30]

These noble and courageous declarations, contained in the appeal sent to the government, reveal better than any other utterance what terms Sergei and the hierarchs about him were willing to offer: they sincerely promise civil loyalty but disclaim all intention on the part of the hierarchy of serving as ecclesiastical police or as guarantors of the political reliability of the clergy either at home or abroad. This is essentially the 'a-political' policy of Patriarch Tikhon, and it is clear that at first Sergei followed it. We have no means of knowing how it happened that he reported the regime's acceptance of this offer. The secrecy with which the Soviets habitually shroud their actions prevents us from knowing or understanding what took place at this time. But the sequence clearly reveals that in the end Sergei's declaration proved far from satisfactory. For it certainly was no capitulation to all the demands of the 'Five' who controlled the ecclesiastical policies of the regime. They acted on the principle — as has already been mentioned — that 'whoever is not with us, is against us.' Accordingly, instead of stemming the persecution, the GPU stepped it up to its highest peak.

As a consequence, arrests of hierarchs broke all previous records: the *émigré* press reported that 117 bishops were exiled at this time, and the whereabouts of forty others were unknown. I visited Moscow during the summer of 1926, and found that ten of the bishops of the patriarchal party had been ordered out of Moscow merely on suspicion of disloyalty. By this systematic weeding out of the best elements of the Russian episcopate the GPU in the end succeeded in purging the Church of all who possessed moral courage to oppose the policies of the state. This then was the process of 'eradication of the best' which goes far in explaining why the Church in the end succumbed to the submissive role it has played ever since.

Sergei himself was again arrested on 13 December (new style) 1926, and remained in prison for three-and-a-half months. He in turn was succeeded in the office of deputy *locum tenens* by Metropolitan Joseph of Nizhni Novgorod, Archbishop Cornelius of Ekaterinburg, and Archbishop Thaddeus of Astrakhan, who subsequently suffered the same fate. Then, contrary to all expectations, Sergei was freed (30 March 1927). Why was this signal favor shown him? Since the official sources are silent even about his arrest (in accordance with the fiction that there had never been any religious persecution in the Soviet Union), it is in vain to search them for an explanation of his release. But a comparison between the 'Declaration' of 29 July 1927 and the document issued on 10 June 1926 (cited above) will shed sufficient light upon this puzzling event, so that we are not wholly in the dark concerning it. During his imprisonment, Sergei decided to yield to the demands of the government and agreed to the terms that were later made public in the now historic 'Declaration.' Thereupon, he became too valuable a tool of the regime's ecclesiastical policy to be kept in prison. Hence he was freed. The government, on its part, true to its opportunistic policy, had previously decided to abandon its support of the anti-patriarchal parties, and now put the policy definitely into effect. For it was clear that the majority of the Russian Orthodox masses supported the patriarchal party. The regime even permitted Sergei to move to Moscow. But he declined and remained in Nizhni Novgorod (or Gorky as the city had been renamed). Sergei's task henceforth was to win the Russian hierarchs and the faithful to the new terms of the *modus vivendi* between the Church and the state, whereby the former was subjugated to the latter

Upon his release, Sergei organized, in May 1927, his temporary Holy Synod from the hierarchs who were willing to support him in the radically new policy, and who were still free to exercise their functions (although many of them were later sent into exile or imprisoned). Among them was Alexei, who became Sergei's successor in the patriarchal office. Others were younger men who were at the time, or shortly before, consecrated to the episcopal office. Sergei likewise once more confirmed (14 June 1927) the dissolution of the Karlovtsi Administration.

Having succeeded in completing the organization of his administration, Sergei then proceeded to issue the 'Declaration,' the terms of which presumably had been agreed upon before he was released from prison. This most important document was addressed to the 'Pastors and the Flock.' [31] Without referring to the letter of 10 June 1926, Sergei once again announced to the Church that with the government's permission he had set up a temporary Holy Synod in May of the current year, and was recognized as the head of the supreme administration of the Church. Accordingly, the Church at last had secured a 'fully legal, centralized administration.' He blamed the recalcitrants, principally the *émigré* clergy, for his and Tikhon's failures to reach this goal earlier. In return he called upon the Church for 'our gratitude to the Soviet government for this attention to the spiritual needs of the Orthodox population.' Such gratitude was to be expressed not merely in words but in deeds as well. 'We wish to remain Orthodox and at the same time to recognize the Soviet Union as our civil fatherland whose joys and successes are our joys and successes and whose misfortunes are our misfortunes.

Every blow directed against the Union, be it war, boycott, or any other common disaster . . . we acknowledge as a blow directed against us.' People who could not understand that it was possible to break with the former regime, and hence who were not ready to co-operate with the Church on this basis, were bluntly told that they 'must either turn about and, leaving their political sympathies behind, must bring to the Church only their faith and work with us only in the name of that faith; or, if they cannot immediately make the change, they must at least cease interfering with us, temporarily refraining from all activity.' Only the relation to the Soviet regime had changed; the Orthodox faith had remained unaltered.

The *émigré* clergy were requested to make a written pledge of loyalty to the Soviet regime, and in case they should refuse or should not keep it, would be 'expelled from the ranks of the clergy subject to the Moscow patriarchate.' It was hoped, the 'Declaration' continued, that this action would 'cause many to pause and consider whether the time has not come to revise their attitude toward the Soviet regime that they may not be cut off from their native Church and land.'

And, finally, Sergei informed the Church that he intended to call the second All-Russian Sobor which would elect the permanent Holy Synod and 'give its final approval, with one mind and voice, to the task undertaken by us in establishing regular relations between our Church and the Soviet regime.'

The differences between this historic document and the letter of the previous year are readily discernible. In the letter, which obviously reflects Sergei's attitude toward the settlement with the regime before he voluntarily changed his mind or was coerced to do so by his imprisonment and the pressure put upon him by the government's agents, he still upheld the position of most of the leading patriarchal hierarchs. For, admitting the necessity of recognizing the Soviets as the political rulers of the land, and interpreting the separation of Church and state in terms of non-interference with each other's autonomous status, he insisted on a policy of a 'free Church in a free state.' It could even be interpreted as a policy of non-co-operation in the political life of the country, and of restricting the Church to its spiritual sphere. But such an attitude proved unacceptable. Hence Sergei's imprisonment, which taught him the lesson.

The Declaration of 1927, on the other hand, clearly shows the change of his position from that of strict separation of the ecclesiastical and the political spheres of activity to one of complete co-operation with, and submission to, the government. It was precisely this change of Sergei's policy against which many hierarchs, who had formerly supported him, now protested. In summing up this aspect of the situation, Troitsky concludes that

Metropolitan Sergei, having submitted himself to the influence of the ober-procurators [he thus designates Tuchkov, Smidovich, Polyansky, and Titlinov], had already abandoned that purely ecclesiastical ground on which he had stood previously, and had assumed the role of a censor of the political tendencies of the clergy abroad; having made this concession, he found it necessary to make even further ones . . . [32]

Furthermore, Sergei laid all the blame for the 'failure' of Patriarch Tikhon to secure the regime's recognition upon the *émigré* clergy and upon those at home who were not in agreement with his new policy. In fact, he asserted that had Tikhon lived a little longer, he would have done exactly what Sergei was now doing. He further declared

the Soviet government guiltless of any wrong-doing in dealing with the Church: its 'distrust of all Church functionaries' was 'just.' Henceforth, the Church has officially and
persistently upheld the fiction that there has never been
such a thing as religious persecution, and all mention of
it has disappeared from its official publications, even from
such as bear the imprint of the patriarchate itself. Russian
Church history has henceforth been written not to tell the
unvarnished and factual truth, but to conform to the current official *dictum* regarding the facts. Thus the government is always innocent of all wrong-doing, and all blame
is placed upon the wrong policies of the Church leaders
themselves, principally upon those under the leadership of
the *émigré* Metropolitan Antony (Khrapovitsky).

The government furthermore demanded that the *émigré*
clergy give a written promise of loyalty. Sergei actually
issued such an order to Metropolitan Evlogy of the West
European archdiocese and the clergy under the latter's jurisdiction.[33] Every priest had to promise to do nothing in his
public capacity 'that might be taken as an expression of disloyalty to the Soviet government.' Evlogy replied that he
and his clergy did not regard themselves as citizens of the
USSR, nor were they so regarded by the Soviet government.
But in order not to break with the Mother Church, he declared himself and his clergy officially a-political, and promised not to permit the use of the churches for political purposes of any sort whatsoever, thus keeping within the limits
of strict neutrality. Sergei accepted this qualified promise
as satisfactory.

Moreover, Sergei well knew and himself acknowledged
that his action in accepting the conditions of 'legalization'
was not valid until it was approved by the next Sobor, representative of the whole Russian Orthodox Church. He and

his Holy Synod possessed only delegated and temporary authority. But although he announced in his 'Declaration' his intention to call such a Sobor (presumably in the near future), no Sobor was actually held until the autumn of 1943; the government refused its consent until then. Even at that time the question of approval of Sergei's 'Declaration' was not submitted for action. Consequently, the far-reaching and basic change of the ecclesiastical policies effected in 1927 by the acting *locum tenens* and his temporary Synod never received the necessary approval in accordance with canonical requirements. Sergei's request that Church schools be opened for persons eighteen years of age — as provided for by the law of January 1918 — was likewise denied by the government. However, the publication of the *Journal of the Moscow Patriarchate* was permitted.[34]

The 'Declaration' caused an immediate outcry on the part of many prominent hierarchs. Of them, some were still in possession of their sees, while most of the others were in prison or in exile. The most courageous among the active hierarchs publicly expressed their disapproval: seventeen of them resigned their sees rather than co-operate with Sergei. They were promptly arrested by the GPU as 'counter-revolutionaries' and were either imprisoned, exiled, or shot.[35] Their sees were quickly filled with appointees favorable to Sergei. Among the protests, the most significant was that of the Guardian of the Patriarchal Throne, Metropolitan Peter himself, who wrote (27 September 1927) from his far-off Siberian exile on the Island of Khe:

For the first bishop, such a declaration is not permissible. I furthermore do not understand why the Synod was organized from such unhopeful individuals who, as I notice from the signatures appended to the Declaration, compose it. Thus, for instance, Bishop Filipp is a formal heretic. I was asked, in more fitting terms, to sign the Declaration, but I did not consent, and was for that reason exiled. I have trusted Metropolitan Sergei, and now I see that I was mistaken.[36]

Since Peter was the Guardian of the Patriarchate, his repudiation of Sergei's act rendered it canonically suspect, if not invalid.

The oldest among the Metropolitans, Kirill of Kazan (who also died in exile in 1936), likewise declared himself opposed to the 'Declaration.' He wrote that Sergei exceeded his authority and encroached upon the very foundations of the Church's polity. Metropolitans Agathangel and Joseph, and Archbishop Seraphim, all three likewise deputies of Peter, protested against Sergei's action. So did Bishop Varlaam of Perm and Evgeny of Rostov.[37]

The protest which received the greatest amount of publicity was the 'Open Letter' of the bishops exiled to the bleak island of Solovky in the arctic waters of the White Sea (27 September 1927).[38] In this forthright document the bishops approve the pledge of loyalty to the government as far as the civil legislation and administration are concerned. They accept 'with entire sincerity' this 'purely political part' of the declaration. But they resolutely protest against the 'categorical and absolute form' in which the pledge is made and characterize it as an 'interpenetration of the Church by the state.' They particularly protest against such phrases as that 'the joys and successes of the state are also the joys and successes' of the Church. For on that basis, they point out, the Church would have to rejoice in the governmental measures for the destruction of the Church. They also protest against the excessively saccharine phrases expressive of gratitude to the state 'for the attention

to the spiritual needs of the Orthodox population,' dryly re-
marking that the sentence smacks of satire. For hitherto,
such 'attention' has taken the form of 'profanation and
destruction of sanctuaries, in the closing of monasteries, the
confiscation of holy relics, the prohibition of catechetical
instruction of children, the removal of religious books from
public libraries, not to mention the deprivation of the
Church of the rights of a juridical person.'

The government [the document asserts] in its legislation as
well as in its administrative measures does not remain neutral
toward the faith, but most resolutely takes the part of atheism,
using all means of governmental leadership to gain its establishment, development and spread as against all religions . . . In
administrative measures the government uses all means toward
the overthrow of religion: it utilizes every opportunity for
closing churches and converting them into places of public
shows; it takes over monasteries, ignoring the introduction of
labor principle into them; it subjects the ministers of the
Church to every sort of discrimination in their economic life;
it excludes the faithful from teaching in schools; it forbids the
circulation of religious books, or books of idealistic tendencies,
by public libraries; it declares by the mouth of its outstanding
representative, that even that limited freedom which the Church
still enjoys is only a temporary measure and a concession to
age-long religious customs of the people. Among all religions,
all of which feel the weight of numberless discriminations, the
most discriminated against is the Orthodox Church . . . [39]

The bishops further complain that they are branded by
Sergei as guilty of counter-revolutionary acts without their
ever having been legally convicted of any such conduct.
They declare such a condemnation of themselves and of
others similarly punished as a denial of the very principle
adopted by the All-Russian Sobor of 1917–18, which stipu-
lated that no bishop or priest is to suffer ecclesiastical cen-

sure or condemnation for holding any kind of political opinion.

And, finally, they point out that the 'Declaration' errs in passing over in silence the important implications of the Law of Separation: this law, they declare,

is bi-lateral: it forbids the intervention of the Church in the political life of the country, but it also guarantees the non-intervention of the government in the Church's internal life and the religious activity of its establishments.

Since the Declaration omits any mention of ecclesiastical autonomy, it in effect surrenders the liberty granted it by the Soviet Constitution itself. This last protest shows better than anything else that the bishops held to the interpretation of the Church-state relationship reflected in Sergei's previous (1926) appeal to the government, and that they were in essential agreement with the terms of that earlier document. It was the radical change of Sergei's position which lost him the previously well-nigh unanimous support of the hierarchs.

Furthermore, the First Five Year Plan, adopted in 1928, included anti-religious aims among the objectives to be gained on the 'cultural front.' Hence it resulted in a heightened attack upon the Church. Article IV of the Constitution of the RSFSR was changed to read that freedom of 'religious confession' was granted to the believers, but freedom of 'propaganda' was restricted to anti-religious organizations and citizens.[40] How this freedom of religious confession was understood may be seen from the supplementary legal explanation issued on 8 April 1929: it consisted of a series of detailed and specific prohibitions restricting the faithful to the bare liturgical service inside the four walls of their churches. Every other activity, no matter how trivial, was expressly forbidden.[41] A little over a month later, the Fourteenth Congress of the Soviets made 'religious propaganda' a criminal offense.

One may gain an idea of the grinding restrictions under which the congregations existed and carried on their work from the memorandum submitted by Metropolitan Sergei to the head of the office for religious affairs, Smidovich.[42] It recites a long list of abuses consisting of excessive financial exactions imposed on the congregations with the view to forcing them out of existence — such as insurance assessments — branding of parish officials as kulaks, refusal of legal protection to clergy, closing of churches at the request of hostile outsiders, registering priests as non-productive social element, levying of exorbitantly high taxes on bishops (one such unfortunate was taxed 10,300 rubles, and had to pay 7,000 rubles toward the *next year's* taxes), denial of educational facilities to children of priests, failure to provide schools for the training of clergy, and the lack of any publication for the use of the patriarchate. It required many years before these abuses were remedied.

A lively account of the persecution suffered by the Russian clergy is afforded by Anton Ciliga, former secretary of the Croatian Communist Party, who was arrested in Russia for 'deviationism' and became acquainted in the Leningrad prison with a number of these 'religious people.' [43] From conversations with his priestly fellow-prisoners, he learned of the opposition to Sergei within the Church, led by the Metropolitan of Leningrad (Joseph, although Ciliga does not name him). This opposition had to do with the so-called 'Josephite' schism, which had occurred in 1928. Joseph had been Archbishop of Rostov, and vicar of the Yaroslavl archdiocese; but he was appointed Metropolitan of Leningrad by Sergei. A short time there-

after, however, he was exiled from the city by the secret
police. This made him a bitter opponent of the regime, and
of Sergei who recognized that regime. Sergei then wanted
to appoint him to Odessa, but Joseph refused, and asked to
be retired. Even though his request was granted, he still
regarded himself as the Metropolitan of Leningrad, and
was so recognized by the two vicars in that archdiocese and
some clergy in Yaroslavl and other archdioceses. For a time
even Archbishop Seraphim of Yaroslavl and Metropolitan
Agathangel joined him. The GPU supported Sergei in this
struggle against the schism and jailed many of Joseph's
adherents.[44]

Ciliga asserts that at the time of his imprisonment (1930),
the Church struggle reached the peak of violence. The majority of the clergy shared with Sergei the conviction that
the future of the Russian Church was indissolubly linked
with that of the state. Accordingly, they were ready to support the state in order to preserve the Church. Those who
did not share Sergei's conviction were dealt with by the
GPU itself. The secret police did not actively interfere
until the opposition, either in the Holy Synod or in the
provinces, grew dangerous to Sergei's control over the
Church. When that stage was reached, the GPU arrested
the disturbers and imprisoned them or sent them into exile.
Ciliga concludes with the interesting reflection that although 'the comedy of the struggle against all religion' was
still being publicly waged by the Association of Militant
Atheists, Stalin was secretly supporting and defending
Sergei's control over the Church.

One wonders how much of this account of the communist author, obviously unacquainted with the finer
points of the ecclesiastical situation, is really correct. But
there is no doubt that it reports what he gathered from his

clerical fellow-prisoners, so that it reflects the mind of the opposition party within the Church. If he is right that the anti-religious drive was a 'comedy,' and that Stalin had already decided to support Sergei in order to convert the Church into a tool of his policy, then it would necessitate the dating of such a radical change of Stalin's ecclesiastical policy some nine or ten years earlier than is usually done.

Comedy or no comedy, the anti-religious drives, particularly those under the direction of E. E. Yaroslavsky, the head of the Militant Atheists, continued without abatement. To be sure, Sergei's biographer, instead of admitting the fact, blandly remarks in referring to this period that 'the loyalty of the Orthodox Church in its relation to the Soviet government raised no doubt in anyone.' [45] Nevertheless, during the years 1929–35, the most determined effort was made to 'liquidate' all religious influences in the Russian society, although at the same time Sergei was granted some opportunities to establish 'legalized' norms of Church life. Parishes were placed under episcopal authority (8 April 1929); the clergy were permitted to organize themselves; obstruction of religious rites was made punishable by a sentence to six months' hard labor.[46]

But side by side with this, and on orders of the government, the Association of Militant Atheists had organized itself in 1925. At first it was small, but by 1929 it numbered over 465,000. The next year it reported the membership of two million — more than a four-fold increase. By the middle of May 1932, the number was reported as 5,673,000. It reached the height of its influence in the early 'thirties. Moreover, the anti-religious publications were widely disseminated. The circulation of the *Bezbozhnik* was in 1931 at its all-time high of 475,500 and the more technical *Antireligioznik* had a circulation of 60,000 (in 1938). By

1933, half or more of the churches were closed. By 1935, Yaroslavsky jubilantly declared that the goal of the anti-religious campaign had been reached. 'There is no use flogging a dead horse,' he asserted.

Sergei, by permission of, or at least by non-interference by, the government, was transferred from Nizhni Novgorod to the see of Moscow (27 April 1934). At the same time he was granted a special title of 'His Beatitude,' which, as the official biographer explains, 'usually characterized the patriarchal dignity in the life and administration of the Russian Church.' [47] In other words, he was granted a rank as close to that of patriarch as was possible under the circumstances. Furthermore, after the death of Metropolitan Peter, the Guardian of the Patriarchal Throne, Sergei succeeded to that title (27 December 1936).[48]

The uneasy truce concluded by Sergei with Metropolitan Evlogy of Paris soon ended in a conflict which resulted in the complete break of relations between the two hierarchs. In 1930 Sergei gave an interview to French reporters representing the journal *Vue*, in which he categorically denied that the Church had ever suffered any persecution from the state. The publication of the interview created a tremendous outcry among the Russian *émigrés*, who branded Sergei's assertion a lie. Evlogy could not successfully shield Sergei from this blunt charge, even if he had been minded to do so. He himself received a letter from a Russian priest in the USSR which informed him of the details of the interview. It had been arranged by the government, which also sent Sergei a prepared statement, to be given out at the interview, and the unhappy man had to sign it. When this became known to the Church people — the priest wrote — they became so violently aroused against Sergei that he was in danger of being mobbed. They denounced him as a liar, and the Synod with the clergy as his accomplices.[49]

The break occurred the same year when Evlogy accepted the invitation of the Archbishop of Canterbury to participate in the prayers held all over England in behalf of the persecuted Russian Church. He decided to go to England. 'While all England will pray for us, shall I remain in Paris as a non-cooperating witness of the single-minded sympathy of all churches with our suffering Church?'[50] Although Evlogy took care to remain politically neutral in all his public utterances, Metropolitan Sergei took him severely to task for having broken his promise given in 1927. Evlogy protested his innocence, but in vain. On 11 July 1930, he was deprived by Sergei of his post as the administrator of the West European archdiocese. However, he refused to obey the order, and placed himself and his archdiocese under the jurisdiction of the Ecumenical Patriarch, Photius II, who made him his Exarch.[51] Sergei thereupon protested against Photius' action.

The extent of co-operation with the government which Sergei practiced (having presumably been compelled to do so by his conviction that the very survival of the Church depended upon it, this hypothesis being the most merciful construction one can place upon his acts) may be gauged by further damning concessions which he and four members of his Synod made during an interview with a correspondent of the official Soviet news agency, 'Tass.' He is reported to have declared that 'in the Soviet Union no religious persecution has ever occurred, nor does it now exist'; that 'churches are closed not by governmental order but because of the will of the inhabitants, and in many cases even the decision of the faithful'; that 'the reports concerning cruelties of the agents of the Soviet government in relation to certain priests absolutely do not correspond to reality and are lies'; that 'priests themselves are guilty of not making use of the freedom of preaching granted them'; and that 'the Church itself does not desire to open theological training institutes.' He furthermore referred to the request of the Archbishop of Canterbury for prayers in behalf of the Russian Church as 'stinking of naphtha' (i.e. as surreptitiously supporting the English desire to control the oil from the Middle East).[52] Such declarations are unlikely except on the supposition that Sergei had to pay the price demanded of him by the state for the meager benefits granted to the Church, but benefits regarded by him as absolutely essential.

A similar attempt to coerce the Russian Church to submit to the Soviet regime was made in connection with the Russian Orthodox Church in America, but failed. This Church was asked by Sergei to give a pledge of loyalty to the Soviet government. But its head, Metropolitan Platon, refused and was thereupon deposed by Sergei for alleged acts of counterrevolution, and the churches adhering to him were declared schismatic. He also dispatched Metropolitan Benjamin to the United States with instructions to take over the administration of the churches. Only a small number of parishes submitted to him. Nevertheless, Benjamin proved himself to be very useful as a Soviet propagandist, particularly through his contributions to the *Daily Worker*.

Although this tragic capitulation of Sergei undoubtedly represented a signal victory of the state over the Russian Orthodox Church,[53] effectively shattering the latter's dream of autonomy, Yaroslavsky's confident assertion that his task of defeating the Church had been accomplished and that it had ceased to exert any influence in society proved to be

an empty boast. When the Soviet government, for the first
time since it had seized power, ventured in 1937 to include
in its census an inquiry into the religious affiliation of the
people, the results revealed that an astonishingly large proportion of the populace still remained loyal to the Church.
According to Yaroslavsky, two-thirds of the adult urban
population declared themselves unrelated to the Church,
while two-thirds of the rural population above eighteen
years of age were Church members. 'Since at the time the
rural population formed 69.8 per cent of the total population, one may conclude that 57 per cent of the adults declared themselves to be believers.' [54] Yaroslavsky thus betrayed the inaccuracy of his own previous claims.

III

It was under such circumstances that what Timasheff
calls 'the Great Retreat,' as applied to the entire Soviet
policy, began in earnest in relation to the ecclesiastical
policy. The beginnings of it, as we have seen, go back to
1927. But the change manifested itself publicly and not
merely behind the scenes in 1936. Finally, in December
1938, it took on the unmistakable characteristics of most
official changes in Soviet policies. The government could
not simply announce the change by an official decree, for
such a procedure would imply that the previous policy had
been wrong; and no such admission could be made, for it
might throw doubt upon Stalin's infallibility, which was
held almost as a dogma. Accordingly, the change was left
to be inferred from the address of a certain Professor
Ranovich, otherwise unknown to fame, who read a paper
before the Academy of Sciences and before the Central
Committee of the Association of the Militant Atheists, in

which he discussed the condition of the early Christian Church. The learned savant undoubtedly startled all — except the initiated few — by asserting that it would be an error to regard early Christianity as a wholly reactionary movement. He had found — undoubtedly after an incredibly arduous research — that the early Christians as a rule belonged to the underprivileged 'toiling masses' and that some were even slaves; moreover, that they held relatively enlightened ideas, and repudiated racial and national discrimination, proclaiming the equality of both slave and free, male and female, rich and poor. As for the conversion of Grand Prince Vladimir of Kiev (987), the professor handsomely admitted — as *Izvestiya* had done before — [55] that the event marked the introduction of higher culture into Russia. Soon after, the Association of Militant Atheists published a pamphlet asserting that Christianity was not to be confused or identified with capitalism and that in fact it had contributed to the improvement of family relations and social customs, and had abolished many harmful practices of antiquity.[56] Later on this same organization went so far as to assert that it had never fought religion, and that the new ecclesiastical policy represented the 'true interpretation of Marxism.' [57]

Subsequently, more definite official acts clearly signalized that the ecclesiastical policies of the regime were indeed undergoing a thoroughgoing transformation. Attempts to liquidate religion were ordered discontinued; public disrespect shown to religious rites received official rebuke instead of support. The seven-day week was restored (June 1940), and Sunday was made the day of rest, despite the Militant Atheists' opposition. Moreover, the grossly and coarsely sacrilegious periodicals, *Bezbozhnik u stanka* and the more 'scholarly' *Antireligioznik,* were discontinued

(1941) 'on account of paper shortage.' Anti-religious museums were likewise closed, and taxes on church buildings,
formerly so high that many congregations had been forced
to surrender them, were reduced.

But the pace of these transformed Church-state relations
was greatly accelerated when Nazi Germany broke its pact
with the Soviet Union and on 22 June 1941, invaded the
territory of its former ally. The regime was now faced not
only with a powerful foreign invader, but also with the
possibility of revolt at home. The problem could be formulated as follows: would the Church people, totaling more
than half of the entire population, seize this opportunity to
go over to the side of the invader, who claimed that he was
coming to 'liberate' the Church; or would they demand the
overthrow of the Soviet regime and help set up some other
sort of government; or, lastly, would they remain loyal to
the Stalin regime? The not-unrealistic fears of the regime
that the Church might choose one of the first two alterna-
tives were quickly dispelled, to the surprise of the regime
as well as of the outside world. The Church remained steadfastly loyal. In fact, Metropolitan Sergei issued, on the very
day that the German armies crossed the Soviet frontiers, an
appeal to the faithful urging them to render the government every possible aid. 'The Church of Christ blesses all
Orthodox who are defending the frontiers of our Fatherland,' he wrote. 'The Lord will grant us victory.' [58] The first
Sunday thereafter he conducted a *Te Deum* for victory in
the presence of 12,000 worshipers, while several thousand
others crowded the yard. Similar services were held throughout the country.

Subsequently, Sergei issued twenty-three proclamations
and appeals, fervently urging his people to render every
sacrifice in the defense of their country. In 1943, these and

other similar official decrees of the Russian hierarchs were published by the government in a sumptuously adorned book entitled *The Russian Orthodox Church and the Great Patriotic War*. The proclamations were couched in fulsome, sycophantic terms. Sergei enthusiastically praised the Soviet regime for the complete freedom granted by it to the Church. He denied that the Church had ever suffered the slightest persecution at the hands of the state, and called upon the people to remain faithful to the regime.

Even a year earlier (1942) the patriarchate had published a book, edited by Metropolitan Nikolai, Exarch of the Ukraine, entitled *The Truth about Religion in Russia*. Fifty thousand copies of this work of propaganda were distributed. In the Preface, Metropolitan Sergei writes:

This book is, first of all, an answer to the 'Crusade' of the Fascists, undertaken by them as if for the 'liberation' of our people and of our Orthodox Church from the Bolsheviks. But at the same time it replies to the more general question: does our Church acknowledge herself to be persecuted by the Bolsheviks and does she ask anyone to liberate her from such persecution?

For those who are convinced of the reality of persecution, the antifascist policy adopted by our Church must appear, after all, forced and contrary to the actual desires of the Church; and our prayer for the victory of the Red Army must appear only a *pro-forma* performance of a duty, or, in other words, a proof of the Church's lack of freedom even within the temple walls.

Referring to the German offer of 'liberation,' Sergei continues:

It is clear that we, the representatives of the Russian Church, cannot even for a moment entertain any thought of accepting any aid or advantage from the enemy's hand . . . It is clear that the Church once for all must identify its fate — for life or death — with the fate of the people . . . For even when the

Church existed under the [tsarist] government, its leaders asserted that she prayed for the regime not in the hope of gain, but in fulfilling her duty revealed to us by God's will [the words of the well-known Metropolitan Filaret of Moscow]. Such also is the position of our Patriarchal Russian Church, in which we differ from all schismatics and schismatizings both abroad and at home.[59]

Metropolitan Nikolai contributed to the book an article entitled 'Freedom of Religious Confession in Russia.' [60] He asserted that the decree of 1918 gives every religious community

The right and possibility of living and carrying on its religious affairs in conformity with the needs of its faith so long as that does not interfere with general order and the rights of other citizens . . . Under the tsarist regime the Church found herself in the service of the government.

The Soviet government's decree concerning freedom of conscience, the freedom of religious confession, removed the yoke which for so many years had lain upon the Church, and freed her from external danger. This resulted in great benefit to the inner life of the Church. The decree grants freedom and inviolability of that freedom to all religious communions.

The greatest benefit accruing to our Orthodox Church consists in the fact that she ceased to be the dominant body, and hence ceased to be a sort of supreme autocratic ruling body, limiting the conscience of other religious bodies.

. . . It is true, as is well known, that anti-religious propaganda is carried on in Russia and its freedom is guaranteed by the Constitution. It is likewise known that the ideology of the Communist party is anti-religious. This is a matter of regret to the Orthodox Church.

But at the same time, it is necessary to assert with complete objectivity that the Constitution, in guaranteeing complete freedom of carrying on religious worship, does not in the slightest obstruct the religious life of the faithful or of the Church generally. . . . No, the Church cannot complain of the government.

But not only did the leaders of the Church speak such amiable words concerning the regime; they proved their loyalty by numerous deeds. For instance, Sergei initiated Church collections for the support of the war; he furthermore provided equipment for a tank battalion named in honor of St. Dmitry Donskoy. More than eight million rubles were contributed for this purpose, not counting the value of the gold and silver objects donated in addition to the money. On Red Army Day in 1942 the Moscow churches and clergy contributed 1,500,000 rubles. The amounts collected all over Russia were often astonishingly large, especially the individual donations. Thus, for instance, Protopriest Andrianovsky contributed 364,720 rubles, while another priest donated 103,280 rubles. The Sverdlovsk congregation is reported to have contributed 2,225,621 rubles.[61] Metropolitan Alexei of Leningrad stated in a letter to Stalin that the total Church gifts in support of war amounted to the enormous sum of 150 million rubles.[62]

Not only Sergei, but other hierarchs and priests showed themselves brave and loyal Russian patriots and defenders of the Soviet regime. Thus Metropolitan Alexei of Leningrad, then holding a see second only to Moscow, and at present the Patriarch of All Russia, rendered distinguished service to the regime during the 900 days of the German siege of Leningrad. He performed his duties with bravery, giving an example to his clergy and his flock in enduring privations and in facing dangers. He was rewarded with the Defense of Leningrad medal. The other member of the triumvirate that dominated the Russian Church at the time, Metropolitan Nikolai (at present of Krutitse, the suffragan see of Moscow), was not only decorated by the government but also appointed to a Special Commission investigating German war crimes.

To be sure, there were cases of defection among the Russian hierarchs, although not many, and they were confined to the German-occupied territories. Thus when Germans invaded the Western Ukraine, Bishop Polycarp (Sikorsky) proclaimed himself head of the autocephalous Ukrainian Church, assuming the title of Archbishop of Lutsk and Kovel. He welcomed the German invaders as 'liberators' of the Ukraine. But a large number of the clergy refused to accept him as their superior. Sergei excommunicated him, depriving him at the same time even of his priestly ordination and declaring all his acts void. Metropolitan Sergei (Voskresensky) of the Lithuanian, Latvian, and Esthonian archdiocese, along with his three bishops, likewise submitted to the Germans. He, too, was promptly deposed. When the Nazis occupied Rostov on the Don, Archbishop Nikolai set up an independent archdiocese there; the same happened in Kharkov, where Metropolitan Theophil went over to the Germans. Both suffered the same punishment as the others.

There was nothing wrong with the patriotism of the Russian clergy and laity — the Russian Church has always shared the fate of the Russian people. What was wrong was that the Church employed canonical condemnations for political offenses. Sergei also used his ecclesiastical office for political pronouncements in respect of the Allies — in blaming or exhorting them in matters purely military or political. His sycophantic glorifications of the 'great, God-given leader of the Russian people' — Stalin — are notorious. The Church thus ceased to be a Church, and became an adjunct of the state. This is the tragedy of the Russian Church and its leadership.

IV

The support afforded the state by the Church was of considerable value. Not only had the Church strengthened the morale of the people, and thus aided both the government and the Army in gaining victory, but by its prompt and swift repudiation of Hitler's offer of 'liberation,' and the excommunication of any Church leader or cleric who defected to the enemy, and by the success in stirring up resistance of the Orthodox population in countries overrun or threatened by the *Wehrmacht*, the Russian Church had rendered the Soviet government invaluable services.

In recognition of these services, an amelioration of the various discriminatory measures occurred even during 1943. The Easter celebration of that year was held openly. The commandant of Moscow lifted the curfew and 50,000 people attended the midnight service. Only about one-third of this number could find room within the thirty Moscow churches still open.[63] Moreover, the famous icon of the Iberian Virgin which formerly had been hung in an outdoor chapel, at the very entrance of the Red Square, was permitted to be placed in the Sokolniky cathedral. It had been kept in the Donskoy Monastery, but was not accessible to the public.

Sergei's consistent loyalty was at last recognized and rewarded by Generalissimo Stalin himself. Immediately after Sergei's return to Moscow from Kuibyshev where he had resided since 1941, he was received, on 4 September 1943, along with Metropolitans Alexei and Nikolai, in an audience by Stalin and Molotov. Sergei is reported to have informed Stalin of the wish of the Orthodox Church to hold a Sobor for the election of the patriarch. Stalin, after expressing 'his approval of the patriotic activity of the Orthodox clergy,' [64] told the three hierarchs 'that there will be no objection from the government' to the election.[65] Was the candidate for the office discussed? We have no information on the point; but it is hardly possible that Stalin would have given consent to the calling of the Sobor without making certain who the next patriarch would be.

A little more light on this important meeting with Stalin is thrown by Metropolitan Nikolai, although one would prefer a more factual and sober account than the rhapsodic description given by his Grace. The only additional detail reported by Nikolai is the assertion that

The head of the government attended, with the same sympathy and extraordinary perception, to all other needs of our Church which we explained to him in that historic conversation.

We, who shared in the reception granted us by Joseph Vissarionovich, live and shall live under the charm of those impressions that overwhelmed us at the time of the meeting, and of the conversation with the beloved Leader of our nation. We were struck with the heartfelt simplicity of the reception and by the personality of the head of the government; for in that outward charming simplicity, in his words, in his dealings with people, we discerned the true greatness of the Leader whom the entire country rightly calls the Great Stalin. Moved and trembling with joy at meeting Joseph Vissarionovich, we were stirred to the bottom of our hearts not only by his understanding of the needs of the Church, but also by his warm concern for the temporal needs of each of us.[66]

Having received permission to hold the Sobor, Sergei proceeded to arrange its sessions. Stalin's consent must have been anticipated, for the hierarchs were already gathered in Moscow not only to greet Sergei, but to take part in the meeting. This is apparent from the fact that four days after the memorable audience with Stalin the Sobor opened its sessions: hence, there could not have been time for sending out invitations or for the journeying to Moscow from any distant place on the part of the invited. Moreover, the Sobor consisted of such a small number of members that this circumstance further explains why it could have been held so promptly. There were only eighteen hierarchs present — a rather sorry commentary on the size of Sergei's party among the Russian episcopate! There were many more bishops in prison or exile than the number that actually participated, although the exact figures are not available.

When the Sobor opened its sessions, Metropolitan Alexei placed only Sergei's name in nomination, on the ground that it was unnecessary to follow the procedure adopted at the first Sobor in 1917. At that time three nominees had been selected and the choice among them had been made by the oldest member of the Sobor, who had drawn the name of one of the three candidates. Of course, by following this method, no one could have been certain which one of the three nominees would be chosen. In the present instance, it seemed highly desirable, in fact imperative, that Sergei be chosen, since he had Stalin's implied or explicit approval — hence Alexei's proposal that the mode used in 1917 be dispensed with. He further argued that 'none of us bishops thinks of any other candidate than the one who has performed so many services for the Church under the title of patriarchal *locum tenens.*' His suggestion was willingly accepted by the assembled hierarchs, who voted for the proposed candidate by crying '*Axios! axios! axios!*' ('he is worthy'), thus signifying their assent by acclamation. Sergei himself then asked: 'Is there no other candidate?' They answered: 'The entire episcopate is unanimous.'

The newly elected Patriarch thereupon addressed the

Sobor, but surprisingly enough, spoke almost exclusively in behalf of the war support, and particularly of the need for collecting money.

Metropolitan Alexei, who plainly revealed himself to be the power behind the patriarchal throne, also delivered a speech, which was entirely devoted to the same theme as that of Sergei. Alexei consciously assumed the role of a Christian patriot and spoke on 'The Christian's Duty toward the Church and the Fatherland.' He asserted that 'our Fatherland with our allies is fighting for truth and right against lie and brutal force,' and expressed his firm faith in 'our ultimate victory over the enemy, in the time-tested spiritual might of the Leader of our Army, and in the strength of our Leader, J. V. Stalin.' He concluded with an impassionate appeal for loyalty and support of the *Vozhd* (i.e. the Leader, *Führer*).

The Sobor thereupon passed a unanimous vote of thanks to the government and an appeal to the world against Hitlerism. It furthermore excommunicated anyone — bishop, priest, or lay person — who 'renounced the faith and the fatherland by going over to the enemy.'

Finally, the Sobor elected a permanent Holy Synod, thus replacing the temporary one appointed in 1927 and subsequently. It consisted of Metropolitans Alexei of Leningrad and Nikolai, the latter of whom was soon to occupy the see of Krutitse (the administrator of the see of Moscow), and of the Archbishops of Yaroslavl, Krasnoyarsk, Kuibyshev, and Gorky (formerly Nizhni Novgorod).[67]

The solemn enthronization of Sergei took place on 12 September, in the presence of 3,000 persons. The cathedral was being repaired and branches of foliage were used to cover up the scaffolding. The new Patriarch walked with Metropolitans Nikolai and Alexei. When Sergei reached the high altar, he took off his mitre and placed on his head the white patriarchal mitre bearing the gold cross — the patriarchal symbol.[68] Sergei frankly asserted that

Nothing was changed when I received the patriarchal rank. Factually, I have borne the patriarchal responsibilities for the past seventeen years. But that was only an outward appearance, and was far from the actual situation. In the position of the Guardian of the Patriarchate I regarded myself as a temporary functionary, and did not fear so strongly the possibility of a mistake. I thought that when the patriarch would be chosen, he would correct the mistakes which had occurred.[69]

In other words, the Patriarch acknowledged that he was merely allowed to change his title. Otherwise his status was not affected.

Was Sergei's election to the patriarchate canonically correct and therefore valid? This is a most difficult question to answer. As we have seen, the rules for the patriarchal election, adopted on 13 August 1917, were not observed by the Sobor of 1943, for then Sergei might not have been chosen, since he would have been one of three candidates.

Furthermore, what immediately strikes one as the most obvious feature of the Sobor of 1943 is the small number of the participants, and the fact that they were all partisans of Sergei, as may be seen from their unanimous vote. Thus the Sobor was plainly a 'packed' meeting. There were only eighteen members, or, as the official biography states, nineteen.[70] But it is a basic canonical requirement that *all* bishops of a given particular Orthodox Church have not only the right but the duty to participate in the Sobor. As far as any published official record goes, there is no indication that the bishops in prison or exile were even invited to the meeting. If religious freedom existed in the Soviet Union — and both the Church and the government have repeatedly and positively affirmed that it did — why then were not *all* Russian bishops invited and in attendance? This appears a grave charge against the canonicity and validity of Sergei's election to the patriarchate, and is the ground of its rejection on the part of the Council of Bishops of the Russian Church Abroad (although the canonicity of that body is even more dubious, to put it mildly). This body regards the Sobor's actions illegal 'because numerous and the most authoritative hierarchs of the Russian Church were prevented from participating in the administration of the Church because they were languishing in exile. Patriarch Sergei cannot therefore be acknowledged as the lawful and fully empowered head of the Russian Church holding the rank of the Patriarch of all Russia.' [71]

It is also to be noticed that the Council did not pass upon the 'Declaration' of Sergei made in 1927, although he then had expressly stated that such an approval was necessary. This important item was not even mentioned or presented for action. Thus the most radical change in the Church's relation to the Soviet state, which at the time when it had been effected had specifically been declared to be of a temporary and provisional character, never received canonical approval.

Another important event occurred on the very day when Sergei was elected Patriarch, but was not even mentioned in the election issue of the *Journal of the Moscow Patriarchate:* the creation of a department for the Orthodox Church Affairs attached to the *Sovnarkom.* Minister G. G. Karpov was placed at its head, and still holds that high post. He was fifty-seven years old at the time, and had devoted most of his life to organizational work for the Communist party and the Soviet government. With him were associated three assistants and a secretary. In an interview with the representative of the Religious News Service, Mr. Karpov informed him that an intricate organization of the department had already been set up throughout the country; more than a hundred such full-time offices had been established, and they in turn had representatives in the local Soviets. According to Mr. Karpov, the function of the department was threefold: contacts between Church and state; preparation of laws and regulations having to do with Church affairs; and the supervision of the execution of the laws.

He furthermore informed the correspondent that many churches were reopened and some repaired, and many priests who had been employed in some secular occupation had resumed their religious calling. Moreover, theological institutes for the training of additional clergy were being planned; one such institute had already been opened.[72] A month later, Karpov announced that religious education of youth was permitted without restriction as to number, although only privately, by parents or priests.[73]

Later, another such department was created for the non-Orthodox religious bodies in the Soviet Union, and was placed under the administration of M. N. Pokrovsky. To be sure, there had existed almost from the beginning a *Sovnarkom* office which had supervised ecclesiastical matters; but now it was openly constituted as a department of the highest administrative organ of the government. In this way, irresistibly reminiscent of the tsarist machinery of a similar nature, namely of the Ober-Procurator of the Holy Governing Synod, the Russian Orthodox Church has been even outwardly linked with the Soviet government. For although the constitutional separation of Church and state continues, yet the newly established office of Minister Karpov clearly betrays the close official connection with the state. An evidence of such pressure may be surmised in an article of Sergei's which appeared in the *Journal of the Moscow Patriarchate* of 7 April 1944 — a month before his death — which was entitled 'Is There a Vicar of Christ on Earth?' Of course, the answer was negative, and since the influence of Roman Catholicism is practically nil as far as the Russian churches are concerned, the importance of this attack upon the Vatican must be sought in the policy of the Soviet state. Later developments made the significance of the action perfectly clear. But we must defer the study of the concrete aspects of this connection to the term of office of Sergei's successor, Alexei. It will then clearly appear that the state has been utilizing the Church as a tool for its own policies. Officially it is claimed, of course, that Karpov's department in no way interferes with the autonomy of the Church's administration. But the instances of overt interferences are so numerous and incontrovertible that the claim is but another example of Soviet duplicity.

Nevertheless, the Church has undoubtedly gained freedom of cult, even though none of the restrictive legislative measures whereby freedom of religion had been severely limited has been repealed. Attendance at church services no longer entails economic discrimination; religious instruction of children is less restricted than before; priests no longer are treated as parasites and deprived of civil rights; and churches are no longer closed on all kinds of pretexts. Even some limited publication program has been allowed, although for the most part it serves the purposes of propaganda.

It would seem, therefore, [writes Professor Fedotov] that the 'New Religious Policy' (NRP) means nothing else but freedom of cult proclaimed in the Constitution of the USSR but never before truly realized. Such freedom, limited as it is, should be welcomed by all friends of the Russian Church and people. Unfortunately, the significance of the change is more far-reaching. Having secured its freedom of cult, the Church by no means limits its activity to the cult alone. Prohibited from carrying the word of God to un-Christian society, the Church sees itself engaged on the political road in the service of the Soviet State. Even limited liturgical freedom had to be bought at a high price.[74]

Among the pressing tasks confronting the Patriarch, the most urgent was that of filling the vacant episcopal sees and thus restoring the regular archdiocesan and diocesan administration. For many bishops were in exile, among them even such as had co-operated with Sergei and yet had for one reason or another displeased the regime. Among these latter were Metropolitans Anatoly of Odessa and Seraphim (Meshcheryakov); Archbishops Yuvenal (Maslovsky) and Pitirim (Krylov) who had been shot; and some quite young bishops, such as Ioann (Shirokov), Seraphim (Aleksandrov), Raphail, Damaskin (Malitsa), Benjamin (Novitsky), and Simon (Ivanovsky), who were in prison or in exile.[75] As the monastic ranks were sadly depleted, Sergei was forced to choose episcopal candidates from among widowed parochial priests and protopriests. Thus he raised to the episcopal rank twenty-seven former 'white' clergymen. Even Metropolitan Gregory of Leningrad belonged to this group. Thereupon, the number of hierarchs reached the total of sixty-six. This figure does not include the bishops who had been deprived of their sees. Of the sixty-six, more than half (thirty-seven) were consecrated in 1944 or subsequently; only six were of earlier consecration (between 1915 and 1928), the oldest among them being the Patriarch himself.

Other important gains for the Church during the remaining eight months of Sergei's life were to be seen in the opening of the Moscow Theological Academy for the training of the higher ranks of leadership, and of the Theological-Pastoral Institute for the parochial priesthood. These were the first legalized schools under patriarchal care, although the Living Church had been allowed some schools; the patriarchal Church had carried on the training of candidates for the priesthood in secret. The curriculum, although reduced in length, did not differ essentially from the previous pattern, except that the study of the Soviet Constitution and of 'social science' were added to the theological subjects. Furthermore, in 1943 the publication of the *Journal of the Moscow Patriarchate* was once more resumed, after a suspension that lasted ten years.

The problems confronting those in charge of the training of candidates for the priesthood were enormous. A. V. Vedernikov, inspector of the Institute, reports that the students, having been trained hitherto in the secularism of the Soviet schools, found the ideas presented to them in the Institute 'foreign' to their ways of thinking. The teachers saw as their most difficult task the 're-education' of their charges. He writes:

The instructors saw before them students who were unlike the former ones who had been brought up from their childhood in the spirit of the Church; these were grown men of the present, not seldom only recently converted to religion and having not the least notion of it save the inner impulse to serve God. It was necessary gradually to lift the ideas of these neophytes to a higher degree of understanding of Christianity as being the supreme religion and the guiding principle of life. This meant first of all a struggle with the tendency of the majority of the pupils toward the learning of theological truths by rote.[76]

Shortly after the election of Sergei, Dr. Cyril Garbett, Archbishop of York, accompanied by two clergymen, the Reverend F. G. House and the Reverend G. M. Waddams, visited Moscow and called upon the newly elected Patriarch to deliver congratulations and best wishes on behalf of the Archbishop of Canterbury as well as of himself. When he was about to return, he was entrusted with a message for the English churches, assuring them that at no time had worship in Russian churches ceased.[77] The Archbishop invited the Patriarch to send a delegation from the Church of Russia to visit England — an invitation accepted and acted upon some years later.

Patriarch Sergei did not long survive his elevation to the patriarchate. He died of cerebral hemorrhage on 15 May 1944, at the age of 78. Three years before his death he had designated Metropolitan Alexei of Leningrad as the Guardian of the Patriarchate. Sergei's own term of office — for thirteen years as deputy Guardian and Guardian, and for eight months as Patriarch — was exceedingly important for the Russian Church. Having begun his leadership of the Russian Church with the intention of securing autonomy for the Church on the basis of the legal separation of the Church from the state, he felt forced to change this policy to one of co-operation with the state in order to insure the Church's survival. This then resulted in his ever-increasing subjection to governmental control, so that in the end but little actual difference could be discerned between the external relations vis-à-vis the Church which had existed under the tsarist regime and that which had existed under the Soviets. Professor Fedotov called this situation 'the new political Byzantinism.' [78] It in turn established the pattern of relations which became not only the fixed form for Russia but for all communist-dominated countries as well. As such, this *modus vivendi*, whereby the Church has been lulled into the belief of the possibility of a 'peaceful coexistence' and of preservation of its essential rights, while in reality it has been used as a tool for eliminating all religion from society, presents perhaps the most difficult problem facing modern Christendom.

NOTES

[1] Nikolai Berdyaev, *Samopoznanie* (Paris, Y.M.C.A. Press, 1949), 153.

[2] Metropolitan Evlogy, *Put' moei zhizni* (Paris, Y.M.C.A. Press, 1947), 197.

[3] Ibid. 157.

[4] Ibid. 195, footnote.

[5] M. Polsky, *Kanonicheskoe polozhenie vysshei tserkovnoi vlasti v SSSR i zagranitsei* (Jordanville, N. Y., Holy Trinity Monastery, 1948), 97. For other particulars, cf. John Shelton Curtiss, *Church and State in Russia* (New York, 1940), 370f.

[6] Metropolitan Evlogy, op. cit. 198.

[7] Polsky, op. cit. 97; Curtiss, op. cit. 13.

[8] *Patriarkh Sergii, i ego dukhovnoe nasledstvo* (Moscow, 1947), 35. This is the 'official' biography.

[9] *Chernaya kniga* (Paris, 1925), 257. There is, of course, no mention of the imprisonment in Sergei's official biography, for it would conflict with the myth that there had never been any religious persecution in the Soviet Union.

[10] Matthew Spinka, *The Church and the Russian Revolution* (New York, 1927), 104ff.

[11] Ibid. 211; Curtiss, op. cit. 168; B. V. Titlinov, *Novaya tserkov* (Moscow, 1923), 20.

[12] Titlinov, op. cit. 20.

[13] Quoted in W. C. Emhardt, *Religion in Soviet Russia* (Milwaukee, 1929), 113.

[14] Ibid. 320. Cf. also Paul B. Anderson, *People, Church and State in Modern Russia* (New York, 1944), 177.

[15] Polsky, op. cit. 98.

[16] *Patriarkh Sergii,* 36.

[17] Metropolitan Evlogy, op. cit. 38–9, footnote.

[18] *Izvestiya* 15 November 1925.

[19] I. Stratonov, *Russkaya tserkovnaya smuta, 1921–1931* (Berlin, 1932), 130.

[20] Spinka, op. cit. 309.

[21] Ibid. 312.

[22] Stratonov, op. cit. 132, 150.

[23] Ibid. 151.

[24] Ibid. 155.

[25] *Vestnik pravoslaviya* (Berlin, 1924). No. 1, p. 58.

[26] *Chernaya kniga*, 257–9.

[27] But compare the report sent by Sergei to Metropolitan Evlogy of Paris, where the negotiations are described (Emhardt, op. cit. 151–3).

[28] It is referred to in S. V. Troitsky, *Razmezhevanie ili Raskol* (Paris, 1932), 93–4; Curtiss, op. cit. 184; the full text is published in French translation in *Russie et Chrétienté* (Paris, 1947), No. 2, pp. 38–41; Anderson's English translation is incomplete (op. cit. 95–6). Moreover, he makes the serious mistake of dating this letter in 1927, thus confusing it with the *second* letter of Sergei, the so-called 'Declaration.'
For my translation of the whole document, see Appendix I.

[29] All these quotations are taken from the text in *Russie et Chrétienté*, op. cit.

[30] *Vestnik russkago Khristianskago studentskago dvizheniya* (Paris, March 1927), 29, quoted in Troitsky, op. cit. 94–5.

[31] The complete text is given in *Patriarkh Sergii*, 58–63; for my translation, see Appendix II.

[32] Troitsky, op. cit. 96.

[33] Metropolitan Evlogy, op. cit. 618–19; also Emhardt, op. cit. 156; Troitsky, op. cit. 78.

[34] Anderson, op. cit. 96.

[35] Polsky, op. cit. 40.

[36] Ibid. 46.

[37] Ibid. Many other protests are cited on pp. 48–57.

[38] The original text in full was published in *Vestnik Russkago studentskago Khristianskago dvizheniya* (Paris, July 1927), 19–20; also partly in Troitsky, op. cit. 87–8; the French translation is found in *Russie et Chrétienté* (1947) No. 2; an English version was published in Anderson, op. cit. 90–94.

[39] Troitsky, op. cit. 88.

[40] Spinka, op. cit. 96.

[41] Ibid. 97–100.

[42] *Poslednyya Novosti*, 3 June 1930; Anderson, op. cit. 106–10.

[43] Anton Ciliga, *The Russian Enigma* (London, 1940), 160ff.

[44] Stratonov, op. cit. 178–80.

[45] *Patriarkh Sergii*, 40.

[46] *Russie et Chrétienté* (1946), 56.

[47] *Patriarkh Sergii*, 41.

[48] Anderson, op. cit. 208.

[49] Metropolitan Evlogy, op. cit. 620–21.

[50] Evlogy, op. cit. 622.

[51] Ibid. 621–7.

[52] Quoted in Troitsky, op. cit. 86–7; Curtiss, op. cit. 265f.

[53] Fedotov, op. cit. 142–3.

[54] N. S. Timasheff, 'Urbanization, Operation Anti-religion and the Decline of Religion in USSR,' in *The American Slavic and East European Review* (New York, April 1955), 232. For different estimates, cf. Robert Pierce Casey, *Religion in Russia* (New York, 1946), 94; also N. S. Timasheff, *Religion in Soviet Russia* (New York, 1942), 65.

[55] Curtiss, op. cit. 274.

[56] Timasheff, *Religion in Soviet Russia*, 114.

[57] Ibid. 118.

[58] *Patriarkh Sergii*, 80; also *Russkaya pravoslavnaya tserkov i velikaya otechestvennaya voina* (Moscow, 1943), 5.

[59] *Pravda o religii v Rossii* (Moscow, 1942), 7–12.

[60] Ibid. 21–6.

[61] *Zhurnal Moskovskoy Patriarkhii* (1945), 46.

[62] Ibid. (1944), No. 10.

[63] *Orthodox Church Bulletin* (London, May 1943), 16.

[64] *Zhurnal* (1943), No. 2.

[65] *Zhurnal* (1943), No. 1.

[66] *Zhurnal* (1944), No. 1.

[67] *Zhurnal* (1943), No. 1.

[68] *New York Times*, 13 Sept. 1943.

[69] *Patriarkh Sergii*, 45–6.

[70] Ibid. 44.

[71] Polsky, op. cit. 71–2.

[72] *New York Times*, 12 August 1944.

[73] *New York Times*, 15 September 1944.

[74] George P. Fedotov, 'Russia's Religious Situation,' in *Christianity and Crisis* (New York, 6 August 1945), 4.

[75] Polsky, op. cit. 41.

[76] *Patriarkh Sergii*, 390.

[77] Ibid. 49; Curtiss, op. cit. 293.

[78] Fedotov, 'Russia's Religious Situation,' op. cit. 3.

III

Patriarch Alexei's 'Strange Alliance'

WHEN Sergei, by the grace of Joseph Vissarionovich Stalin, the second Patriarch of Russia, died on 15 May 1944, there existed not the slightest doubt as to his successor. The dynamic and ambitious Metropolitan Alexei of Leningrad and Gorky, who for a long time had been 'the power behind the patriarchal throne,' was the obvious choice. So when the members of the Holy Synod assembled immediately after the Patriarch's death to be apprised of his successor, they could not have been unprepared for the content of Sergei's letter, dated 12 October 1941. He had written:

In the event of my death, or of the impossibility of my performing the duties of the Guardian of the Patriarchate, this duty in its entire scope as to the patriarchal rights and responsibility shall devolve upon the Most Reverend Metropolitan Alexei Simansky.[1]

We should bear in mind that not only was Alexei the oldest among the Russian hierarchs in the order of their consecration, but also by all odds the one favored by the regime and the most prominent and influential among his fellow-bishops. It was only natural that he should be chosen for the high office.

Thus Alexei's appointment to the post of the Guardian

of the Patriarchal Throne caused no surprise either to him or to any other member of the Holy Synod. Since it had been made almost three years prior to the Patriarch's death, Metropolitan Alexei had ample time to prepare himself for the exalted role he was destined to play. From his subsequent career it appears fairly safe to assume that during the intervening period he indulged in ambitious dreams. For he intended to revive the ancient aspiration of the Russian Church for pre-eminence among the Eastern Orthodox communions, which went under the slogan of 'Moscow-the-Third-Rome.' When in 1453 Constantinople had at last succumbed to the assaults of Sultan Mohammed II, and the Byzantine Empire had thus finally received its *coup de grâce*, it was the Russian Tsar, Ivan III, who claimed to be the heir of the Byzantine imperial rank. Ivan had married Sophia, the niece of the last Byzantine emperor, and through her claimed to inherit the imperial dignity symbolized by the double-headed eagle. Along with the aggrandizement of the state, he likewise sought to raise the Church to a corresponding dignity, for at the time the latter ranked only as a metropolitanate. Since the Ecumenical Patriarch of Constantinople, the highest dignitary among the Eastern patriarchs, was then a mere functionary of the Turkish Sultan, and moreover, since the Russians considered the Byzantine Church as having betrayed Orthodoxy by accepting the Florentine Union (1439), the Russian Church seemed in their eyes as the logical and rightful claimant to the leading position among the Orthodox Churches. The theory embodying this claim, known as 'Moscow-the-Third-Rome,' was first formulated by a monk, Philotheos. He developed it in a letter addressed to Tsar Vasily III, Ivan's son (1505–33), and it quickly became part of the official tsarist policy. It claimed that the hegemony of Christendom, forfeited both by Rome and Constantinople, had passed on to Moscow, which thus secured the headship of all Christendom, or, at least of the Eastern Orthodox Churches.

In Patriarch Alexei this ancient dream found its modern exponent, although necessarily in a changed form, since there were no Orthodox tsars any more. And not only has he been able to realize that dream to a surprising degree; what is even more astonishing, he has found effective support for its realization in the Soviet government itself. The latter, however, lends its aid for reasons other than either Philotheos or Alexei ever imagined.

I

Sergei Vladimirovich Simansky (Alexei's 'lay' name) was born in a cultured and well-to-do bourgeois ('aristocratic,' in the words of his official biography) [2] Moscow family on 27 October 1877. He studied for eight years at the Moscow Lyceum of Tsarevich Nicholas. Upon graduating, to satisfy the wish of his parents, he matriculated in the law faculty of the University of Moscow, although he himself wished to choose the ecclesiastical career. He wrote his graduating thesis on 'Combatants and Non-combatants in Time of War,' and received his degree of candidate in law in 1899. Thus the present head of the Russian Church possesses legal training.

After a year's interlude, during which he served in the army, he at last could gratify his original desire by entering the Moscow Theological Academy, located at the historic and famed Trinity-Sergei monastery. He spent four years in this institution of higher theological learning. Since it is most unusual for a university graduate with a law degree to

enter a Theological Academy — normally, most of its students come from priestly seminaries — young Simansky was
looked upon as an outsider. But he apparently knew well
what he wanted. In the middle of his theological course he
decided to become a monk. He was then twenty-five years
old. It must be remembered that in the Eastern Orthodox
Churches the hierarchical career is reserved exclusively for
monks, and that ordinarily in preparation for this career
the higher theological education, offered only in the
Academies, is required. The parochial clergy (the so-called
'white,' in distinction from the monastic, 'black' clergy) is
married, and therefore not eligible to episcopacy. Thus
young Simansky, who on the occasion of his receiving the
monastic habit at the hands of the Academy rector assumed
the name of Alexei, had decided earlier than usual to seek
this exalted career in the Church. For the monastic vow
was commonly professed on the part of Academy students
just before their graduation. The next year he was ordained
a hieromonk (i.e. a priest-monk, or as the Roman Catholics
would say, a 'regular priest'). He thus placed his foot on the
lowest rung of the ladder by which he was to climb up to
the patriarchal throne.

The first post to which he was appointed, after his graduation in 1904, was that of the inspector of the Pskov
Theological Seminary (a training school for the 'white'
priesthood). Two years later, having been elevated to the
rank of archimandrite, he received a similar post in the
Tula and subsequently the Novgorod seminaries. Bishop
(later Metropolitan) Evlogy of Paris, who met Alexei while
the latter was rector at Tula, speaks of him, with evident
disdain, as a dandy wearing 'a scented, silk, rustling robe,
and delighting in his worldly elegance.' [3] Alexei's promotion thereafter was astonishingly rapid: in 1913 he already

had secured the episcopal rank, having been consecrated in the St. Sophia Cathedral of Novgorod as the Bishop of Tikhvin. Six hierarchs officiated at this ceremony, among them even the Patriarch of Antioch, Gregory VI, who happened to be visiting Russia at the time. As Bishop of Tikhvin and vicar of the Novgorod archdiocese, Alexei actually exercised the functions of the archdiocesan administrator.

The era of the First World War was a tremendously important period for Russia and, as later events were to prove, for the world as well. For the radical political forces of the time, which in the end overthrew tsarism, were then struggling for supremacy. Our official source for Alexei's life says nothing about the young bishop's attitude toward the politics of the time. His ecclesiastical opponents, on the other hand, fill the lacuna with somewhat scanty, but nevertheless concrete, information which gives some hint as to why the official biographer preferred to say nothing about it. We are informed (on a somewhat dubious, and certainly unfriendly authority) that when Bishop Alexei served as vicar of the Novgorod archdiocese, he became a member of the Rasputin Petrograd circle and through this notorious connection secured an audience with Empress Alexandra. Also he was a protégé of the Grand Duchess Elizabeth Feodorovna, who presented him with valuable gifts.[4]

We possess no information whatever as to his conduct during and after the Revolution of 1917. But since the next event which is mentioned is his transfer, in 1921, to the important post of the first vicar of the Leningrad archdiocese with the rank of the Bishop of Yamburg, it may be safely inferred that he had successfully weathered the revolutionary storm and that he enjoyed the confidence of both Metropolitan Benjamin of Leningrad and of Patriarch Tikhon. In fact, it was the former who personally chose

Alexei as his first vicar. In May 1922 Alexei, along with Bishop Nikolai, became the actual administrator of this archdiocese, the most important ecclesiastical see after Moscow. Metropolitan Benjamin was soon arrested for his stand against the usurpation of the patriarchal powers by the Living Church leaders. He had excommunicated Archpriest Vvedensky, who took the leading part in usurping the supreme administration of the Church. For that offense Benjamin was placed on trial and sentenced to death. Thereupon, Bishop Alexei, who had stood apart from the proceedings against Benjamin, now quashed the condemnation of the Living Church,[5] although after this event even he is recorded as being among those sent into exile.[6] His official biography naturally does not mention anything so derogatory to him. In fact, it asserts just the opposite.[7]

The rapid rise of Bishop Alexei to the highest rank in the Russian Church was greatly aided by his elevation, in 1926, to the archiepiscopal dignity as the head of the Novgorod archdiocese. After Tikhon's death, Alexei was appointed a member of the Holy Synod by Metropolitan Sergei. He thus shared in the responsibility for the basic and radical decision taken in 1927 by Sergei to establish a *modus vivendi* with the Soviet government. In 1932 he was raised to the rank of the Metropolitan of Novgorod and the next year was transferred back to the see of Leningrad. From this exalted post he had but one more step to make — to the patriarchal throne.

When Leningrad was besieged by the German army during World War II, Metropolitan Alexei remained with his flock throughout the 900 days of the siege, sharing sufferings and privations. He barely escaped death when one Easter the Germans bombed the church where he had but a short time before celebrated the liturgy. He zealously supported Metropolitan Sergei in the latter's patriotic appeals in behalf of the war effort. During 1941–2 Alexei collected 3,182,143 rubles in his archdiocese and contributed, besides, 500,000 rubles toward the organization and equipment of the tank battalion St. Dmitry Donskoy, one of Sergei's projects. His war pronouncements were not a whit behind those of Sergei in patriotic fervor and devotion to Stalin. No wonder, therefore, that after Sergei's death he should have succeeded to the post of the *locum tenens* of the patriarchate.

II

Alexei's first act in his new post significantly took the form of a letter to Stalin, in which he pledged to the 'God-appointed Leader' his unswerving loyalty. This document, dated 19 May 1944, is so characteristic of the unbelievably changed Church-state relations in the Soviet Union that it is worth quoting in full. It is addressed not in the formal, official manner to Marshal Stalin, but in the intimate, friendly fashion to 'Dear Joseph Vissarionovich.'

Our Orthodox Church has unexpectedly suffered a heavy trial: Patriarch Sergei, who has administered the Russian Church for eighteen years, has passed away.

You well know with what wisdom he bore that laborious duty. You are acquainted with his love for the Fatherland, his patriotism which inspired him during the past war period. To us who were his closest collaborators, his feeling of the most sincere love and devotion to you, as to a wise, God-appointed Leader over the peoples of our great Union (that was his own actual expression) were well known. That feeling showed itself with unusual force after he had become personally acquainted with you on the fourth of September of the past year. Not a few times have I heard him recollect with tender feelings that meeting. He also attached a high, historic significance to your regard for the needs of the Church, a regard most valuable to us.

With his passing, our Church was orphaned. But by the will of the late Patriarch, God has willed that I should take upon myself the duty of the Guardian of the patriarchate.

In this most responsible moment of my life and my ministry in the Church, I feel the need to express to you, dear Joseph Vissarionovich, my personal feelings.

In the task confronting me I will be steadfastly and inflexibly guided by the same principles which characterized the ecclesiastical career of the late Patriarch: on the one hand, I will adhere to the canons and regulations of the Church; and on the other, [I will adhere] with steadfast loyalty to the Fatherland and to you as the head of its government.

Co-operating fully with the Council for the Affairs of the Russian Orthodox Church, and along with the Holy Synod established by the late Patriarch, I shall be protected against making mistakes and taking false steps.

I beg you, deeply honored and dear Joseph Vissarionovich, to accept these my assurances with the same good faith with which I make them, and to believe in my feelings of deep love and gratitude to you, by which all Church functionaries are inspired who are from henceforth to be guided by me.[8]

This remarkable document plainly reveals the course which Alexei proposed to follow. Be it said to his credit that he skillfully places the canons and the regulations of the Church before loyalty to the fatherland and to Stalin. But on the other hand it should be noted that despite the loudly proclaimed non-interference of the state in Church affairs, Alexei promises to co-operate with the governmental officials for ecclesiastical affairs in order to be 'protected against making mistakes and taking false steps.' That phrase gives the game away!

Alexei's first two letters to the Church are concerned altogether with the war and its support by the clergy and the lay people: 'We will be firm to the end, fathers and brethren, and will let no weariness or doubt concerning the victory of truth paralyze or lessen our endeavors!' [9]

His public activity was likewise predominantly of a patriotic and political nature, as even his official biography bears witness. He issued three appeals in behalf of a fund for widows and orphans of Red Army soldiers, and made a beginning of it by contributing one million rubles, as he announced to Stalin.[10] When the second front was opened in Western Europe, he appealed to the Archbishop of Canterbury for prayers on behalf of the Allies. He likewise wrote to Metropolitan Benjamin of North America to 'transmit to the leaders of the American public our hearty wishes for the [success] of the united armies in their military operations in northern France.' [11] He also encouraged the Rumanian Church to agitate for the breaking of their country's ties with fascist Germany and the going over to the side of Russia's allies. Alexei made a similar appeal to the Bulgarian Metropolitan Stephan, encouraging him to support the newly formed National Front (dominated by the communists), so that his country might thenceforth act 'in complete unity with the great governments of Russia, England, and America!' [12] The new *locum tenens* conceived of the 'separation' of Church and state in the Soviet Union in a rather surprising and paradoxical way!

Alexei found an enthusiastic supporter of his progovernmental policy in Metropolitan Nikolai of Krutitse, the suffragan bishop of Moscow; the latter consequently occupies to this day a position second only to the Patriarch himself. Nikolai lustily joined in the chorus of praises for Stalin and all things Soviet — a role in which he has eminently distinguished himself. On the occasion of the twenty-sixth anniversary of the October Revolution he contributed

an article to the *Journal* extolling Stalin to a degree rarely
exceeded by the most notorious communist sycophants:

Our Church members, along with the entire population, discern in our Leader the greatest [man] that has ever been born
in our country. For he unites in his person all the characteristics mentioned above in connection with our Russian
bogatyrs [ancient heroes] and the great military leaders of the
past [Alexander Nevsky, Dmitry Donskoy, Prince Pozharevsky,
General Suvorov, and Field Marshal Kutuzov]. Our people see
in him the incarnation of all that is best and brightest; all
which represents the holiest heritage of our Russian nation
bequeathed to us by our ancestors. In him are indissolubly
united the fervent love of the Fatherland and of the nation,
the most profound wisdom, the strength of a manly and firm
spirit, and a fatherly heart . . .

The name of Joseph Vissarionovich Stalin, surrounded by the
deepest love of all nations of our country, is the banner of
glory, culture, and greatness of our Fatherland! [13]

To be sure, Alexei, despite all his preoccupation with
political and patriotic affairs, did not altogether neglect the
interests and duties of his ecclesiastical office, particularly
in view of the forthcoming Sobor for the election of the
Patriarch. Continuing the practice of his predecessor, he
filled the episcopal vacancies with new appointees chosen
mostly from among elderly widowed priests and archpriests
(since monks were not available); thus during the nine
months before the Sobor actually met he consecrated six-
teen new bishops. The total number of Russian hierarchs
then reached fifty (exclusive of those in prison or exile).

The episcopal conference for the arrangement of the
Sobor was held on 21 November. Aside from the principal
task, the assembled bishops also learned of the opening of
many additional churches throughout the country, and par-

ticularly of the inauguration of the Moscow Theological Academy and the Moscow Theological–Pastoral Institute. The publication program had also been extended.

But the great event during this early period of Alexei's leadership of the Russian Church was, of course, the Sobor for the choosing of the successor to the late Patriarch. Not that the outcome had ever been in the least doubt in his mind or the minds of any others. But it was an opportunity to derive as much benefit from this rare and solemn occasion as possible. And Alexei made the most of it.

III

The Sobor which met on 31 January 1945 in the Voskresensky Cathedral in Sokolniky (a suburb of Moscow) was a magnificent and brilliant affair. For besides the Russian hierarchs who were in attendance, the heads of almost all the autocephalous Orthodox Churches were present. Hence the Sobor, comprising an imposing array of the highest ecclesiastical dignitaries from the Orthodox lands, or their representatives, had the appearance of a Pan-Orthodox Council. The Russian contingent consisted of four metropolitans, thirteen archbishops, twenty-nine bishops, three archimandrites, two hegumenoi, sixty-eight archpriests, eight priests, six hieromonks and deacons, and thirty-eight laymen. It was led into the Cathedral by Metropolitan Benjamin of North America and the Aleutian Islands. But despite this large number, it did not comprise all Russian bishops, for many were still in exile or in prison. Thus the Sobor was not really representative of the entire Church, but only of the partisans of Alexei. The non-Russian delegates comprised Patriarchs Christopher of Alexandria, Alexander III of Antioch, and Catholicos-Patriarch Callistratos of Georgia; Metropolitan Germanos, who represented the Ecumenical Patriarch of Constantinople; Archbishop Athenagoras, representing the Patriarch of Jerusalem; Metropolitan Joseph, representing the Church of Serbia; and Bishop Joseph of the Church of Rumania. They were accompanied by twenty-six other delegates. Although the foreign dignitaries had no official part in the election of the Russian Patriarch — for the Russian Church was properly jealous of its auto-cephaly — yet they undeniably added splendor and dignity to the occasion such as had never been displayed at any other patriarchal election in the entire history of the Russian Church.

Besides these high-ranking ecclesiastical dignitaries, the government was represented by its Minister, Georgi G. Karpov. The Sobor was opened with a word of greeting delivered by Metropolitan Alexei, which was immediately followed by that of Karpov. In his speech, which clearly stated what the government expected of the Church, Karpov graciously acknowledged the patriotic devotion of the Church to the government during the war, and paid a particularly appreciative tribute to 'that wise old man, Sergei.' He further declared that

In our own days, when the Hitlerite brigands have villainously attacked our sacred soil, when all the peoples of the Soviet Power in a mighty surge rose to the great Patriotic War for their honor, freedom, and independence, the Orthodox Russian Church from the very first day of the war most ardently joined in the defense of the Fatherland, using all means and possibilities at its disposal.

The patriotic activities of the Church have found expression not only in messages and church sermons, but also in collections and donations to build tanks and planes and to relieve the sick, wounded, invalids and orphans. The government of the Soviet Union has regarded and regards with profound sympathy measures of the Church aimed at assisting the struggle against the enemy.

In our great country, with the victory of the new, hitherto unknown in the world and most equitable socialist regime, new mutual relations between the Church and the state have been created. The Great October Revolution, which set free our people, also liberated the Russian Orthodox Church from the fetters that once hampered and constrained its internal activities. Freedom of conscience, proclaimed by the Decree of January 23, 1918, was guaranteed by the basic law of our country — the Soviet Constitution. The Council for the Affairs of the Russian Orthodox Church of the Council of People's Commissars of the USSR, created by a governmental decision, maintains a bond between the government and the Patriarch of Moscow and All Russia in affairs requiring governmental decision. While interfering in no way in the internal life of the Church, the Council contributes to the further normalization of relations between the Church and the state, supervising the correct and prompt execution of the laws and decrees of the government concerning the Russian Orthodox Church.[14]

One rather wonders what this high official of the Soviet government was doing among Orthodox hierarchs, and what business he had in welcoming the delegates. Nor was this an isolated instance of such governmental representation at purely ecclesiastical gatherings. The official record shows that it became a standing procedure.

The first thing on the agenda was the adoption of a loyal address to the government, moved by Metropolitan Nikolai and carried unanimously. In fact, all proposals put forth at the Sobor were carried unanimously. This was followed by greetings from Patriarch Alexander III of Antioch and by the ratification of the new ecclesiastical administrative regulations.

Since no session was held the next day, the election of

the Patriarch took place on the third day, 2 February. The outcome of the procedure caused no surprise; after all, there was only one candidate, and he had the government's approval! Moreover, the Minister of that government was right there in the meeting! Since not a single dissenting vote was registered, Metropolitan Alexei was elected Patriarch of Moscow and All Russia by a 100 per cent vote, thus exceeding in respect of percentages even the best-managed governmental elections. Thereupon, the Sobor broke out into a jubilant, thrice-repeated '*Axios!*' ('he is worthy'). Metropolitan Nikolai, who conducted the procedure, then read the act of election. Thereupon, after a solemn *Te Deum,* and the reading of two messages by the newly elected Patriarch, the Sobor was concluded to the satisfaction of all.

The enthronization was held on 4 February, after which splendid ceremony Patriarch Alexei received the congratulations of all the Eastern Orthodox hierarchs present — apparently that was the extent of their participation — followed by that of Minister Karpov. Thereupon, *mirabile dictu,* Karpov and Alexei embraced and thrice exchanged kisses! Wonders never cease!

One of the messages read by the Patriarch after his election was an appeal to the Christians of the world. In it, Alexei reminded them of the heroic sacrifices and victories of the Red Army:

The Russian Orthodox Church, the Church of the great country which has borne the brunt of the blows of bloodthirsty Fascism and has wounded it mortally in battle, through the voice of the Council of all Bishops, numerous clergy and laymen addresses you, brother Christians, with an appeal to complete the holy struggle. Let us complete the holy enterprise of the destruction of Fascism in the same spirit of close unity and fraternal mutual aid.

Warrior Christians, let us not flag in our heroic effort — the enemy is still strong! [15]

The rest of the address likewise dealt almost exclusively with the war theme and was essentially political. To read it without the knowledge of where and when it was delivered, one would hardly guess that it was adopted at a solemn religious ceremony!

The festivities were continued in the evening by a banquet at which the distinguished guests were present, including Karpov, who received a special invitation from the Patriarch. Karpov, in turn, entertained the foreign guests the next day, on which occasion the Patriarch was present. On 6 February a concert was held in the great Hall of the Conservatory in which both the Patriarchal Choir and the State Symphony Orchestra participated.

The imposing façade of the Sobor to which the distinguished foreign guests had obviously been invited for the purpose of adding pomp and circumstance, showed on closer examination ominous cracks. For although Alexei secured for the patriarchate an acknowledgment, on the part of the other autocephalous Orthodox Churches, of the legitimacy of his administration, this action had no canonical validity. It must be remembered that the so-called Sobor of 1923, which deposed Patriarch Tikhon and abolished the patriarchate, also had the approval of the Ecumenical Patriarch, Gregory VII, and other Eastern patriarchs, an approval which did not validate the action of that spurious Sobor. Alexei, unfortunately, did not succeed any better than his predecessor in securing the approval of the disaffected Russian hierarchs for the radical change of the ecclesiastical policy adopted in 1927. As has already been pointed out, Sergei's act was not regularized either by the Sobor of 1945 or by any other, although Sergei himself had admitted the necessity of its approval by a future Sobor. Moreover, the Sobor of 1945 was not attended by *all* Russian bishops (nearly 100 at the time), for many were still in prisons or in exile. That in itself rendered it irregular from the canonical point of view.

IV

Furthermore, the subsequent course of action pursued by Patriarch Alexei seriously raises the question whether the attendance of the Eastern patriarchs and the other heads of the autocepalous Churches at the Sobor was not in part a premeditated plan to bind these bodies closer to the Moscow patriarchate with the view to securing ultimately the Russian hegemony of the entire Orthodox East. The journeys throughout the near East later taken by the Patriarch or his emissaries 'to return the visit,' and particularly the assembling in Moscow of what amounted to a Pan-Orthodox Council in 1948, lend color to such an interpretation. Nor was the significance of this aspect of Alexei's course of action lost on the other Churches, especially the Constantinopolitan, Jerusalemite, and the Greek. For they promptly recognized in it the revival of the 'Moscow-the-Third-Rome' tradition.

Moreover, such a course of action was of obvious political advantage to the Soviet government, which thus extended and strengthened its influence over the 'satellite' and other Orthodox countries. Surely astute politicians like Stalin and his 'Ober-Procurator' Karpov, were fully and keenly aware of these political implications! One need not even guess at it, for the proof that Stalin had his fingers deep in the ecclesiastical pie was soon forthcoming.

Hence, it is not difficult to perceive in what valuable

and effective ways the Russian Orthodox Church has been
helpful to the Soviet regime: in respect of the internal
situation, the bishops or other ecclesiastics who had been
opposed to, or were even merely non-co-operative with, the
regime, were removed from their sees. Their places were
then taken by others, often servilely subservient to it.
Moreover, the Church was exceedingly useful in securing
and maintaining the loyalty and submission of the Russian
population itself. For many hierarchs and clergy — although not all — exerted themselves to the utmost by means
of direct instruction in the duties of a Christian citizen, by
numerous appeals, and by regular prayers for the government in every liturgical service, to instill loyalty into the
hearts of the faithful. Equally important was the service of
the Church in respect of world opinion. For the Church has
never tired of denying, officially and categorically, that
there was or had ever been the least religious persecution
in the Soviet Union; and has asserted with even greater
positiveness that there exists full liberty of conscience and
freedom of the Church. In these ways, as Professor Schmemann writes, the state is able to carry on its propaganda

to resanctify it in the eyes of the West, which is sensitive to
religious persecution. I should like to add that public opinion
in the West was 'duped' rather easily by the religious 'renais-
sance' in the USSR.[16]

In these, and other ways to be mentioned later, the Church
has proved itself once more, as it had been in the tsarist
days, an important pillar of the state.

No wonder, therefore, that the government on its part
showed itself increasingly favorable toward the Church.
And in the dire condition in which the latter found itself,
the help of the state proved indispensable. Among the
Church's needs the greatest was that of securing trained

clergy, both parochial and monastic. For during the years
when the Orthodox Church had been under an active attack
by the regime, the ranks of the clergy and of the monastics
had been frightfully depleted: in 1914 the lay membership
of the Orthodox Church was estimated at 117.4 million.[17]
It was divided into 67 dioceses with 130 bishops and with
54,174 churches; but not all of these were parish churches,
and 5,830 were not in use. Thus the functioning parish
churches numbered 40,437. The clergy of all grades (not
including the bishops) numbered 50,105. There also existed
550 monasteries with 21,330 monks and novices, and 473
convents with 73,299 nuns and novices.[18] There existed 58
seminaries for the training of the priesthood. In 1916 the
state contributed to the support of the Church 62,920,835
rubles and more than one half of this sum was a subsidy for
the parochial schools. In 1940, the Soviet Press Bureau reported that there still existed — but on a somewhat larger
territory — 4,225 churches served by 5,665 priests under 28
bishops.[19] Hence, slightly more than 10 per cent of the
number of churches and about 11 per cent of the clergy of
all grades survived the appalling rigors of the terrible years
between 1914 and 1940. And those are official figures, representing, since 1927, years when the Church was sup-
posedly absolutely free and unhindered! Furthermore, since
there existed no schools for the training of the priesthood,
there was a desperate need of securing new and trained
clergy for the parishes.

Patriarch Alexei, therefore, obtained an audience with
Stalin (10 April 1945), of which we possess an ecstatic, eye-
witness report from the pen of the eloquent Metropolitan
Nikolai: 'The conversation was an intimate talk of a father
with his children,' he assures us.[20] It centered about the
need for more schools for the training of the clergy and

about the establishment of a patriarchal press. The Patriarch asked for eight more schools (two already existed), and in the course of the next three years he got them.[21] But he also discussed with Stalin and Molotov (who was present at the interview) his intended visit to Jerusalem ('to visit the Holy Sepulchre,' he was supposed to have said) and to other Near Eastern countries. Surely the Patriarch did not need Stalin's permission merely to visit the Holy Sepulchre! But if one assumes that the discussion really concerned the ways in which the Patriarch could secure leadership over the other Orthodox Churches, then it becomes clear why the subject was discussed with Stalin. And no wonder that the latter approved all Alexei's plans!

When by the end of 1953 the ten schools for the training of the clergy were reported upon, they consisted of two Academies for the higher theological studies and eight seminaries for the training of parochial priesthood.[22] Likewise, the number of churches was very considerably increased, some closed ones having been reopened. In 1946, the patriarchate reported the number as 22,000, which is obviously a guess rather than an exact count. All Russian 'statistics' are likely to be in 'round numbers,' and therefore not statistics at all. One must remember that even statistics must serve the cause of the revolution. But if the number may be accepted as approximately correct, then it would represent a fivefold increase gained in the space of six years. It was also reported that in 1948 there existed 89 monasteries in the Soviet Union. The number of bishops in 1950 was officially given as 73, although three years earlier the *Great Soviet Encyclopedia* states that there were 83 of them.[23] The French Catholic periodical, *Russie et Chrétienté*, published in 1949 the list of Russian episcopal dioceses and reports that there were then 74 hierarchs

(3 metropolitans, 24 archbishops, and 47 bishops).[24] From another source (but apparently no more accurate than the others) we learn that the number of the clergy rose to 30,000, which would be more than a fivefold increase. But this figure is suspect in the highest degree. For the theological schools certainly did not graduate some 25,000 students by 1953, i.e. within the eight years of their existence — as this figure would presuppose — and there is no mention in the *Journal* of any such extraordinary number of priests ordained without theological training.

Among the other gains secured by the Church were the relaxation of the law against the religious instruction of children in groups of more than three (although, significantly, the law itself was not repealed), and the permission to engage in a moderate amount of publishing. A patriarchal press was set up and a monthly publication, the *Journal of the Moscow Patriarchate,* was revived (for it had been published previously). From time to time a book or some devotional material made its appearance. It has recently been reported that a new translation of the New Testament from the Greek is being prepared — and what is particularly interesting, that this project is carried on with the help of the British and Foreign Bible Society in Paris. But some years ago when the American Bible Society offered $90,000 worth of portions of the Bible to the Russian Church, even though the gift was at first gratefully accepted and the boxes were stacked on the New York pier according to instructions received, it was in the end declined by both the government and the Church on the ground that the Russian people were well supplied with Bibles!

V

The most significant of Patriarch Alexei's policies, as has already been alluded to, was his decision to cultivate close relations with the other Eastern Orthodox Churches. This program, as we have seen, had Stalin's personal approval, and plainly appears to be a part of the plan of the Soviet government to extend and consolidate its influence and control over the Orthodox countries by means of ecclesiastical relations. Thus whatever is beyond the power of the Soviet political, economic, or military influences is to be accomplished by ecclesiastical means, since the countries of the Near East are, for the greatest part, Orthodox in religion. And since Alexei's own ambition of securing for Moscow — i.e. for himself — hegemony among the Eastern Orthodox Churches coincides with these political aims of the Soviet regime, the Church and state can work hand in glove to gain these objectives. Thus the Patriarch, ostensibly on the pretext of returning the visit of those heads of the Orthodox Churches who had participated in the Sobor for his election, pursued his own and his government's aims. The time-honored pre-eminence of the Ecumenical Patriarch was challenged by Alexei in a most serious manner.

Leaving Moscow on 28 May in company with Metropolitan Nikolai and Archbishop Vitaly, Alexei was bidden farewell at the airfield by Minister Karpov. He began his 'historic pilgrimage' in Jerusalem, where he was received with a fitting ceremony by Patriarch Timotheos. This was the first time in history that a Russian Patriarch had personally visited the Holy City — or for that matter any other of the Eastern Orthodox Churches. Alexei paid his respects to the Holy Sepulchre, and made pilgrimages to Bethlehem, Jordan, and many other holy places. But the fulsome official report of his visit says nothing about the subject of his conversations with Timotheos. Nevertheless, if one does not know positively what the hidden motive of the visit really was, one may be allowed to make a guess. It is a well-known fact that the Patriarch of Jerusalem with his whole hierarchy occupies a precarious position: for his flock with the parochial clergy is solidly Arab, while the hierarchy is exclusively Greek. There has existed a tension between the Greek shepherds and the Arab flock for many decades — a tension by no means lessened by the creation of the new state of Israel. During the tsarist days, much of the financial support of the patriarchate was derived from the numerous Russian pilgrims flocking annually to visit the Palestinian holy places. The Russian Imperial Palestine Society also greatly contributed to the support of schools and other establishments of the patriarchate. With the fall of tsarism, both of these sources of income dried up. But recently the Soviet government secretly resumed the subsidy of the patriarchate of Jerusalem. Is it too far-fetched to suppose that Patriarch Alexei was the bearer of the tempting offer of financial aid from Stalin, which His Holiness, Patriarch Timotheos, found irresistible?

On 6 June Alexei and his suite proceeded to Egypt, where at Cairo they were received by Patriarch Christophoros. The two patriarchs 'confirmed the great necessity of unity, both in the present and the future.' [25] Passing on to Alexandria, Alexei had an audience with King Faruk. He likewise accepted the local Russian Orthodox colony into communion with the Moscow patriarchate, thus inaugurating the policy of taking the Russian churches abroad directly under his own jurisdiction. The official account records that this event signifies the beginning of the penetration of the light of Russian Orthodoxy throughout the world! [26]

From Egypt Alexei started on his return trip. But *en route* he made stops at Beirut in Lebanon and later at Damascus, Syria. At the latter place, which is the seat of the patriarchate of Antioch, he was received by Patriarch Alexander III. Again the subject of discussion between the two patriarchs is not stated in the official account of the visit. But since the patriarchate of Antioch — the only Arab-dominated see among the four ancient patriarchates — is ostracized on that account by the Greek Churches, and thus can hope for no aid from them, it had long been the beneficiary of the Russian Imperial Palestine Society. When the tsarist regime fell, and the support was consequently withdrawn, the Antiochene patriarchate found itself in grave difficulties in attempting to keep its schools open. We learn that the Soviet regime has since provided subsidies to the patriarchate. Again, is it not reasonable to suppose that Alexei was the intermediary between the Soviet government and Alexander III in negotiating the arrangement whereby Antioch is pledged, in return for the subsidy, to support Alexei's ambitions as well as the Soviet schemes for the Middle East domination?

From Damascus Alexei proceeded in a special plane furnished by the Soviet authorities by way of Teheran, Baghdad, and Baku to Moscow. It is noteworthy that although the Ecumenical Patriarch had been represented at the Sobor of 1945, the Russian Patriarch neither called on him in person nor sent anyone else to do so. Why this omission, unless it was tacitly acknowledged by both patriarchs that the real aim of the journey was the wresting of the pre-eminence from the patriarchate of Constantinople?

Alexei did not remain in Moscow long, for in October he

undertook another journey, this time to neighboring Georgia, to return the visit of the Catholicos-Patriarch Callistratos.

The remaining Orthodox Churches had to be satisfied with the visit of a delegation of high-ranking members of the Russian hierarchy. Thus, in April 1945, the Bulgarian Exarch, Stephan, received a visit from the Russian delegation headed by Archbishop Gregory of Pskov. The Bulgarian Church, long regarded as schismatic by the Ecumenical Patriarch and the Greek Churches, was at last received into communion with the Constantinopolitan Patriarch on 22 February 1945.

The visit of the ecclesiastical delegation of the Moscow Patriarchate in Bulgaria was converted into a great ecclesiastico-political event, which contributed greatly and fruitfully toward the pacification of the Bulgarian nation at the critical moment of its political life.[27]

Here we have a frank acknowledgement of the ulterior significance of the 'ecclesiastical missions.' Exarch Stephan returned the 'courtesy' call in June 1945 and was greeted on this occasion by both Alexei and Karpov.

At the same time, another delegation was sent to Yugoslavia. It was headed by Bishop Sergei of Kirovgrad, and was received by Metropolitan Joseph of Skoplye, for Patriarch Gavrilo was still held in a Nazi concentration camp in Germany. In view of the subsequent relations between the Soviet Union and Yugoslavia it is interesting to note that the delegation had an audience even with Marshal Tito, 'who in the interview underscored the immense role of the Russian and the Serbian Orthodox Churches in their active co-operation with their people during the war with fascist Germany.'[28] By his command, Patriarch Alexei and Bishop Sergei were awarded high Yugoslav orders, while the rest of the delegation received minor decorations. Moreover, one of the Serbian bishops let the cat out of the bag as far as the ulterior significance of the Russian visit was concerned by declaring: 'It is necessary to agree that among all the nations professing the Orthodox faith, only the Russian nation can stand at the head of historic Orthodoxy.' [29] Whether such a declaration was spontaneous or officially inspired, I leave to each man's fancy.

Finally, a delegation headed by Bishop Yeronym of Kishinev and Moldavia was sent to Rumania. It was received by the old and feeble Patriarch Nikodemus, who was handed a written message from Patriarch Alexei containing 'questions and conditions concerning the establishment of fraternal relations between the Russian and the Rumanian Orthodox Churches.' [30]

Besides these 'fraternal' visits, Patriarch Alexei's program comprised the recall to his obedience of the Russian Churches abroad. This included not only the Churches of the Baltic states of Esthonia and Finland, which were visited for that purpose by Metropolitan Gregory of Leningrad and Gorky. But an attempt was made to restore to the Moscow jurisdiction the far-flung Russian Churches in Western Europe and North America. Thus the principal Russian hierarch assigned to the task of foreign relations, Metropolitan Nikolai of Krutitse, was sent, with a suitable delegation, to London. The visit was in response to the invitation of the Archbishop of Canterbury, and in return for the visit to Moscow by Dr. Garbett, the Archbishop of York, in September 1943, shortly after the election of Sergei to the patriarchate.[31] The Russian delegation was met at the Waterloo station by Archbishop Garbett, who represented the Archbishop of Canterbury; by a deputy of Metropolitan Germanos of Thyateira, representing the

Ecumenical Patriarch; and by several others. They were entertained at the Lambeth Palace by Archbishop Temple, and received in audience by King George VI.

On his way from England, Metropolitan Nikolai visited Paris in order to negotiate the conditions of submission on the part of Metropolitan Evlogy of the Western archdiocese of the Russian Church, who since his break with Metropolitan Sergei had been under the jurisdiction of the Ecumenical Patriarch. In this task he was temporarily successful. Nikolai likewise succeeded in securing the submission of Metropolitan Seraphim, who belonged to the Russian Church Abroad (formerly known as the Karlovtsi Administration), the group most resolutely opposed to the Soviet government and therefore to the Sergian-Alexian Russian Church.[32] A similar signal victory was won by another delegation sent to Germany, where another member of the above-mentioned body, Archbishop Alexander, accepted the jurisdiction of Alexei.

Upon his return to Moscow, Metropolitan Nikolai triumphantly reported that all schismatic movements of the Russian Churches abroad had been terminated.[33] But this was not quite correct. For the head of the recalcitrant body, Metropolitan Anastasy, had refused the appeal to return to the Moscow obedience and obdurately remained in opposition to it. In fact, in May 1946, he organized in Munich the Council of Bishops of the Russian Orthodox Church Abroad, comprising some twenty-six episcopal members. Judging from the frequent condemnations of Anastasy in the *Journal of the Moscow Patriarchate*, Alexei finds it hard to accept his defeat. Moreover, by the time Nikolai made his boastful assertion, Metropolitan Evlogy of Paris had once more withdrawn from Alexei's jurisdiction.

Other delegations were sent to Prague, Vienna, Harbin, and Budapest, and each on its return reported a successful accomplishment of its mission.

A similar attempt was made in connection with the Russian Church in North America, which was under Sergei's sentence of 'suspension.' When that Church was invited to send a delegation to the Sobor of 1945, Metropolitan Theophilus appointed to it Bishop Alexei, Archpriests Joseph Dzvonchik and N. Metropolsky, and Attorney Ralph M. Arkush. The two first-named left ahead of the others. Then without warning Mr. Arkush's visa was cancelled on the ground that only clergy were permitted to attend the Sobor. Moreover, Bishop Alexei and Father Dzvonchik in Siberia were required to transfer from their plane to a train, and arrived ten days too late. Nevertheless, they held several conversations with the Patriarch afterwards. The chief stumbling block was the Patriarch's demand that the members of the American Church 'refrain from criticism of the USSR.' [34]

Archpriest Dzvonchik, one of the delegates, urged that as citizens of the United States, American Russians could not pledge loyalty to any other government. Moreover, the delegation insisted that the Patriarch recognize the autonomous status of the American Church. But Alexei refused to yield on either of these points, and on 16 February handed the delegates his *Ukaz* in which he once more demanded that the Americans abstain 'from political activity against the USSR,' and that they elect a new Metropolitan who, however, must be confirmed by the Patriarch. He further reserved the right to reject the Metropolitan 'for any reason whatsoever.' [35] These conditions were decisively rejected by the Council of Bishops which met in Chicago in June 1945 under the leadership of Metropoli-

tan Theophilus. Thereupon (September 1945) Archbishop
Alexei of Yaroslavl and Rostov was dispatched to America
by the Patriarch to negotiate with the American episcopate.
He held his first conference with Metropolitan Theophilus
and Archbishop Vitaly on 28 October, but accomplished
nothing. In fact, the Church held a Council in Cleveland
(1946) and declared itself completely autonomous, although at the same time requesting the Patriarch 'to continue the American Church in your fold and be our spiritual head under conditions preserving completely autonomy as it exists at present.'[36] The Patriarch then lifted the
ban, and sent Metropolitan Gregory of Leningrad and
Gorky to the United States (July 1947) to reopen the
negotiations. The latter remained in this country for three-
and-a-half months. But since he still persisted in imposing
the old terms, and the American Church by that time was
quite determined not to submit, Theophilus did not even
respond to Gregory's overtures. Thereupon, to the surprise
of all, Patriarch Alexei declared his willingness to accept,
to a considerable degree, the decisions of the Cleveland
Council, with the exception of the autonomy of the American Church. But Theophilus resolutely rejected this concession, whereupon the negotiations collapsed. Gregory
returned to the Soviet Union by the end of November.[37]

In still another category stands the 'reunion' of the
Ukrainian Uniate Church of Galicia. This Church, which
had been cut off from the Orthodox Russian Church by
the Union of Brest in 1596, was 'brought back' to the
Mother Church exactly 350 years later — in 1946. The
event was undoubtedly inevitable, but the manner of its
accomplishment was reprehensible. It was initiated in
December 1945 by a letter of the Orthodox Metropolitan
Ioann, the Exarch of the Ukraine. He declared that the

only true Church is 'the Graeco-Eastern Church,' of which the Russian constitutes a part. Thereupon the rest was accomplished, in ways strongly reminiscent of the well-known communist device of the fifth column, by a small group of the Uniate clergy organized into what was called 'the Initiating Party for the Reunion of the Graeco-Catholics with the Orthodox Church.' They were headed by Archpriest Dr. Gavril F. Kostelnik and the hieromonks Mikhail N. Melnik and Antony Pelevetsky, all three of whom had gone over to the Russian Orthodox Church in Kiev. Two of them, Mikhail and Antony, had been raised to the episcopal rank by Metropolitan Ioann and had been assigned dioceses among the Uniate population. These three men formed a 'cell' which, with the generous support of the government, seized the leadership of the Uniate clergy. Thereupon, a Council under the presidency of Kostelnik and his two episcopal conspirators was held in Lwov (8–9 March 1946), and was attended by 204 priests and 12 laymen. This 'packed' meeting duly repudiated the Union of Brest of 1596 and voted, in behalf of the five million Galician Uniates, an appeal for reunion with 'the Mother Church.' The appeal was addressed not only to Patriarch Alexei but to Minister Karpov as well! What business did Karpov have with the reunion of the Uniates, if the Russian Church were absolutely free in its internal affairs?

Another letter was addressed to Stalin which declared:

Three hundred fifty years ago the imperialist Poland of the gentry, striving to increase the enslavement of Ukrainian lands that had been forcibly separated from the mother country, also broke the religious and ecclesiastical unity of those lands in the East of the same race and religion with the help of proud and power-loving Rome, which had always dreamed of its own dictatorship in the Christian world.

. . . Under your great leadership, what seemed to be an un-attainable dream for which the best generations of the Ukrain-ian people had fought, has come true. All the Ukrainian lands, from the Tissa across the Carpathians and from the San up to the Don, from the Pinsk swamps up to the Black Sea, have been reunited.

In our new free life, feeling ourselves independent masters of our land, we have cast off the moral yoke that had been forced on us against our will and for our destruction. The assembly of the Uniate Church of the Western Ukraine, having gathered in Lwov, decided today, March 8, 1946 [mistakenly 1945] to abolish the Brest union with the Vatican established in 1596 [mistakenly 1595] and to return to the bosom of the Holy Russian Orthodox Church of our forefathers, whose light shone from Kiev, Russia, historic cradle of the Russian, Ukrain-ian and White Russian peoples . . .[38]

Needless to say, the 'voluntary' request of the Ukrainian Uniates was granted! But one may judge of the temper of the infuriated Ukrainian Uniates, on whose behalf it was ostensibly made, from the fact that the chief promoter of the 'reunion,' Archpriest Gavril F. Kostelnik, was assassi-nated by them at the door of the church (20 September 1948), just as he had completed the celebration of the liturgy there. The *Journal* tendentiously suggests that the assassin, who committed suicide, was a German-Ukrainian nationalist instigated to his murderous deed by the Vati-can.[39]

The Vatican sharply condemned the high-handed pro-cedure at Lwov, pronouncing it invalid, and charging that the Uniate Metropolitan Slepoi and four of his bishops had been imprisoned. Moscow acknowledged the arrests, but claimed that the five Uniate hierarchs had been col-laborating with the German invading armies.[40]

Similarly, in 1949, the Sub-Carpathian Ruthenian Uni-ates were 'reunited' with the Moscow patriarchate, as the result of the efforts of Archbishop Makary of Lwov. The next year the Czechoslovak Uniates followed suit.[41]

Another aspect of the same policy of expansion of the Moscow jurisdiction may be clearly seen in the case of the Czechoslovak Orthodox Church. This exceedingly small body (organized in 1921)[42] was artifically 'blown up' to the size of a full-grown exarchate of the *Russian* Orthodox Church as early as April 1945, when the Russian Archbishop Elevfery of Rostov and Taganrog was appointed its Exarch. This Church had never, throughout its short history, been under Russian auspices, but had been the daughter of the Serbian Orthodox Church. Now it was bodily taken over by the Russians. The reason for the obviously exaggerated promotion of this numerically insignificant body to the rank of exarchate can be readily understood: it was to serve as a counterweight to the overwhelmingly predominant Roman Catholic Church in Czechoslovakia. In short, the Russian Exarch was set up to hold the balance against the Czech Roman Catholic Archbishop.

But this was not enough: on 10 January 1946, a Czechoslovak delegation, headed by the native administrator of the archdiocese, Archpriest Čestmír Kračmar, arrived in Moscow and humbly petitioned to be received under the patriarchate's jurisdiction. The delegation was met at the airfield by Karpov's deputy, the vice-chairman of the Council, S. K. Belyshev, and after a dinner at the patriarchal residence, was entertained at a dinner by Karpov and Belyshev. Of course their request was graciously granted, so that it could not henceforth be said that the Czechoslovak Orthodox Church had been unceremoniously taken over by the Russian patriarchate.[43] This intermediate step toward the aggrandizement of the Czechoslovak archdiocese reached its ultimate goal in October 1951 when it was granted autocephaly by Alexei, who thus acted as if he already possessed the rights of the Ecumenical Patriarch! It thus joined the family of Orthodox Churches and became theoretically on par with any of them, including even the Russian Orthodox Church itself! Why, in heaven's name, was this done? Was the purpose merely to set up a Church in Czechoslovakia which could combat the Roman Catholic Church? Or was it done to create another autocephalous Slavic Church in order to increase the Slavic, Russian-dominated preponderance within Orthodoxy against the Greek and other non-Slavic Churches? Or is this the first actual assertion of hegemony on the part of the Moscow patriarchate, for canonically no Church may be granted autocephaly without the consent of all Orthodox Churches, particularly that of Constantinople? Some such pattern is certainly emerging, so that one can confidently affirm that there is method in the madness.

Furthermore, in July 1946, no less a person than Minister Karpov himself visited Czechoslovakia and was received, along with Exarch Elevfery, by the already ailing President Beneš as well as by the communist members of the government, Nejedlý and Kopecký. What his business was, the official report does not say.[44] But I happen to know on the best of authority that Karpov had a private interview with Patriarch František Novák of the Czechoslovak National Church, urging him to submit his Church to the jurisdiction of the Moscow patriarchate. That Church is by no stretch of the wildest imagination an Orthodox one. In fact, in its initial period, when under Dr. Farský's leadership it sought to find an ecclesiastical roof over its collective episcopal head in the Serbian Church, it was declared heretical. For theologically it is a Unitarian body. This, of course, was of no importance to Karpov, whose only interest was the increase of the Russian ecclesiastical influence in Czechoslovakia against the Roman Catholic Church. Moreover, is it not surprising that Karpov should have conducted the negotiations when an Exarch of the Russian Church, in the person of Elevfery, was available? What a commentary on the claim that the Russian Church is absolutely free from governmental interference in its internal affairs!

Another rather remarkable thing in this connection occurred on 6 July of the same year when Exarch Elevfery celebrated a solemn requiem for John Hus at Tábor. Why this farce? Does the Russian Orthodox Church claim Hus for its Reformer, in the same way as such highly educated communists as Nejedlý acclaim him as an early fighter for social justice in behalf of the toiling masses? Or is this a transparent attempt to play upon the nationalist susceptibilities of the Czechs in order to 'soften' them in favor of communism and Russian Orthodoxy?

The pattern established in Czechoslovakia was followed, two years later, with the Orthodox Church of Poland. Patriarch Alexei granted autocephaly to this Church on 22 June 1948, and announced this act of usurpation to the Ecumenical Patriarch, Athenagoras. Similar negotiations regarding the granting of autocephaly by the Russian Patriarch have been carried on for some years with the Orthodox Church of Finland, but so far without definite results.

But all this extensive and intensive program of visitation abroad on the part of Patriarch Alexei, his chief deputy in foreign relations, Metropolitan Nikolai, and the rest of the missions abroad, was by no means a 'one-way traffic.' Most of the heads of the Near Eastern Orthodox Churches quickly discerned the wisdom of keeping in the good graces of their ecclesiastical neighbor who had so suddenly risen

to a position of great power and influence. The visits to
Moscow were inaugurated by the Bulgarian Exarch Stephan
(27 June 1945); [45] and he was followed, in October, by the
aged Rumanian Patriarch Nikodemus, who 'half constrained [by Groza], half willingly, undertook the journey.' [46] And in every instance when an ecclesiastical delegation came to Moscow, it was greeted not only by the
patriarchal authorities, but invariably by Karpov or his
deputy as well.[47] Alexei repaid Nikodemus' visit the next
year. When he conducted a church service in Bucharest,
there were officially present not only the members of the
Rumanian government, but of the Russian Embassy as
well. Church attendance must be looked upon as a strange
duty for the communists! The Parisian delegation, led by
Exarch Seraphim, came to Moscow early in 1947.[48] A little
earlier the Albanian delegation arrived to ask Alexei for
assistance, which was promised them. Later in the year
came the mission of the Hungarian Orthodox Church. This
body had petitioned, as early as 1945, for the privilege of being received under the jurisdiction of the Moscow patriarchate. Now they came to secure the fulfillment of their
petition, and it was granted. There is no explanation why
this particular Church had to wait so long for the desired
boon.[49] This unmistakable recognition of the Moscow patriarchate as the dominant see of Eastern Orthodoxy cul-
minated, in 1950–51, in the visits of four Eastern patriarchs:
the Catholicos-Patriarch Callistratos of Georgia came in
July; four days later arrived the Bulgarian delegation,
headed by the acting Patriarch Kyrill (who was soon after
elected Patriarch); that same evening the delegation of the
Rumanian Church made its appearance, with the new
Patriarch, Justinian, a former member of the Communist
Party,[50] at its head; and later Patriarch Alexander III of

Antioch arrived, and was for about a month the guest of Alexei at the latter's 'dacha' near Odessa. In addition, the newly installed head of the Albanian Orthodox Church, Archbishop Paissy, shared the honors. Karpov or his subordinates were, on several occasions, among the hosts. Is it too much to infer, from all these visits, that His Holiness, the Patriarch of Moscow and All Russia, is already treated with all the deference due to the actual head of Eastern Orthodoxy? Alexei's dream of realizing the 'Moscow-the-Third-Rome' tradition is already being fulfilled.

But if his claims are accepted by some autocephalous Orthodox Churches (be it noticed that all, with the exception of the Patriarch of Antioch, belong to the 'satellite' nations, and that he is a Russian 'pensioner'), opposition to him from some Russian ecclesiastical groups is as strong as ever. One of the most interesting of such outbursts, published anonymously in a mimeographed form by a Russian priest most probably belonging to the party of Metropolitan Anastasy, and republished by Professor A. V. Kartashev in Paris,[51] merits close attention.

Russia at present needs above all else *truth* and *freedom* [he writes], and she will secure freedom only by way of truth. As long as we lie, we will be slaves, witnessing to our slavery and strengthening it by our lies. That is why our confessors and martyrs of the last ten years have led us toward freedom, while the hypocrites and liars of our day lead us into slavery. [p. 3]

Thereupon, the author recounts the various ways in which the leaders of the Church reacted toward the Soviet regime:

Some became martyrs. Others hid in the emigration or in the underground — the forests and ravines. The third group went underground — the individual souls who learned the wordless and almost invisible secret prayer, the prayer of hidden fire . . . At present there has appeared a fourth group: they decided to tell the Bolsheviks, 'Yes, we are with you!' And not only to tell them, but to say and confirm it by deeds; to help them, to serve their objectives, to fulfill all their demands, to lie along with them, to participate in their deceits, *to work hand in hand with their political police* . . . [p. 7]

We have seen these people. They all have the typical, stone-masked faces and clever eyes. They do not restrain themselves, but openly lie, and that about the most serious and sacred [subjects] — the situation in the Church and the confessors martyred by the Bolsheviks. In their own peculiar way they made their agreement with the Soviet regime, and not troubling themselves about observing the ecclesiastical canons, they 'chose' from among themselves a 'patriarch' acceptable to the Bolsheviks, and officially announced a new, religiously paradoxical and unheard of 'Soviet Church' . . . [p. 8]

With that consciously false announcement Alexei, and later his emissaries, went abroad. They knew better than anyone else that the Church became a *submissive establishment of the Soviet regime:* that they were in duty bound and must speak only that lie, and yet they persisted in lying 'about the real freedom of the Church' . . . [pp. 9–10]

Such were the performances of his [Alexei's] political emissaries in Paris, of those so-called 'metropolitans' and 'bishops.' The same thing occurred in America . . . [p. 10]

And later these 'hierarchs' appeared among us . . . and demanded that we acknowledge their 'authority' and submit to their *ecclesiastical* leadership in the same way in which they submitted to the Soviet *spiritual* leadership. But of this latter they kept still . . . [p. 12]

In answer to such as have forgotten or have become weary, we affirm the thesis: Orthodoxy, which has subjected itself to the Soviets and has become the tool of the world anti-Christian seduction, is not Orthodoxy, but a seductive anti-Christian heresy which decks itself in the torn garments of historic Orthodoxy . . . If someone really does not see the false role of the new 'patriarch,' let him but consider: himself enslaved, WHY does he [Alexei] strive to subjugate to himself and enslave along with himself even the Orthodox Church abroad?

Himself having accepted the compromise with the enemies of Christianity and Orthodoxy . . . WHY does he force that compromise upon us who, God be praised, yet have the possibility not to pray for the devil and his successes in the world? . . . Why has it suddenly become necessary to deprive the Orthodox abroad of their freedom of prayerful and ecclesiastical breathing? [p. 13]

Here is a downright and categorical denial of the official sycophantic chorus surrounding the Moscow patriarchate!

VI

If there should still remain a lingering doubt as to the goal which Patriarch Alexei, under the vociferously denied but clearly apparent aegis of the Soviet government is pursuing, any such doubt must surely vanish when one observes the Patriarch's obvious efforts to gain primacy among the Eastern Orthodox Churches. Thus, for instance, in September 1947, Alexei called a conference to Moscow, at which representatives of most of the autocephalous Eastern Orthodox Churches were present. The aim of this meeting was the calling of an ecumenical Council for a thorough re-examination of the Orthodox canons. The last such generally acknowledged Council had been held in 787 — the Seventh Ecumenical Council of Nicaea. Although attempts had been made by the Patriarch of Constantinople in the nineteen-twenties to arrange for such a meeting — for the need for it had long been felt — he had found it impossible to carry out his plan, for the Turkish government of Mustapha Kemal Pasha had refused permission to hold it. When Alexei assumed the initiative in this matter which clearly belonged to the Ecumenical Patriarch, the latter protested. Thereupon, the Russian

Patriarch postponed the contemplated gathering until later.

The desired opportunity presented itself the next year, on the occasion of the celebration of the five-hundredth anniversary of the autocephaly of the Russian Church. This historic event was fittingly commemorated in a magnificent assemblage of ecclesiastical dignitaries representing most of the Eastern Orthodox Churches, and lasted ten days from 8 to 18 July 1948. This imposing gathering, convoked to Moscow by Patriarch Alexei, could be regarded as a veritable Pan-Orthodox Council, as the Serbian Patriarch Gavrilo asserted it to be.[52] As such, it is of tremendous significance not only for Russia, but for the entire Orthodox East. It was attended in person by three patriarchs (not counting Alexei): the Catholicos-Patriarch of Georgia, Callistratos, the Patriarch of Serbia, Gavrilo, and the Patriarch of Rumania, Justinian. Three other patriarchs sent their representatives: the Ecumenical Patriarch was represented by Germanos, Metropolitan of Thyateira; the patriarchs of Antioch and Alexandria shared in being represented by Alexander, Metropolitan of Emessa. Each of these principals was accompanied by a suite. Besides, the delegation from Bulgaria was headed by Exarch Stephan; the Church of Greece, by Metropolitan Chrysostom; the Church of Albania, by Archbishop Paissy; the Church of Poland, by Archbishop Timothy. Also the heads of the four Russian exarchates and of the other missions abroad were in attendance.

The Conference dealt with four general topics: Orthodoxy and the Papacy; the Validity of the Anglican Orders; the Church Calendar; and Orthodoxy and the Ecumenical Movement. But even in this instance one cannot be certain to what degree these subjects represented the genuine interests of the Church, and how far they represented the political concern of the government bent upon attacking the West, especially the Vatican. At any rate, the best one can say is that in this case the interests of the Church and the state strangely coincided.

The first of these subjects was fairly exhaustively presented in a number of more or less able and objective studies, the writers of which agreed that the papacy is and has ever been an inveterate enemy of Orthodoxy. In the Resolutions adopted at the plenary session it was decreed that the papacy has

sullied the purity of the ancient universal teaching of Orthodoxy by the new-fangled dogma of the 'Filioque,' the Immaculate Conception of Our Lady, and especially by the completely anti-Christian teaching on papal supremacy in the Church and papal infallibility.

For that reason the Conference now pronounces

a condemnation of the Roman Papacy because of its newly formulated Roman dogma, which represents a purely human invention and which has no foundation either in Holy Scripture, Holy Tradition or in the writings of the Fathers of the Church and in Church history.[53]

The Roman Church is further condemned for being a political organization inimical to the interests of workers.

At the present time also the activity of the Vatican is directed against the interest of the workers. The Vatican is the centre of international intrigues against the interests of the peoples, especially the Slav peoples; it is the centre of international Fascism.

Moreover,

The Vatican . . . is one of the instigators of two imperialistic wars, and at the present time is taking a very active part in instigating a new war and, generally speaking, is involved in a political struggle with world democracy.

It may be noted that the gravamen of these charges centers about political, rather than theological, matters. In this feature one may easily discern the government's interest in the struggle against Roman Catholicism. Karpov even advocated the adoption of the 'federal' or 'national' polity of Eastern Orthodoxy as the exclusive form of ecclesiastical organization for the entire Christendom, because of its 'autocephalous' character. From his point of view, the national Orthodox Churches could be far more easily controlled than the absolute and centralized Roman Church.[54] Hence, the assignment to the Russian Church to fight the papacy.

The problem of the Anglican Orders gave the members of the Conference much more trouble. For the Churches of Constantinople, Jerusalem, Cyprus, and Rumania had recognized the validity of Anglican ordination, the last-named as recently as 1935, although with certain conditions and reservations. Moreover, the Anglo-Catholic party within the Anglican communion had made declarations as to their doctrinal beliefs which had satisfied the Orthodox. But the difficulty was that this group was only a part of the whole Church, and the other Anglican parties did not share their opinion. Moreover, the Thirty-nine Articles, despite the disclaimers of the Anglo-Catholics, still had to be regarded as the Church's official confession of faith, and they did not bear out the Anglo-Catholics' position. What was needed, therefore, was a positive and unequivocal *official* statement of faith wholly consonant with the doctrine of the Orthodox Churches, particularly on the sacraments, and among them especially on the necessity of the episcopate in apostolic succession. Since no such official declaration has ever been made, 'the Orthodox Church cannot agree to recognize the correctness of Anglican teaching on the Sacraments generally and on the Sacrament of the Priesthood in particular, neither can she recognize the validity of Anglican ordinations which have actually taken place.' The *sine qua non* of the recognition is then stated as follows:

. . . We declare that the present Anglican hierarchy can receive from the Orthodox Church recognition of the grace of her priesthood, if, as a preliminary, there is established between the Orthodox and the Anglican Churches, a formally expressed unity of faith and confession as indicated above. When once such longed-for unity is established, recognition of the validity of Anglican Orders can be accomplished in accordance with the principle of Economy by the only authoritative decision which we recognize — the 'soborny' decision of the Holy Orthodox Church.[55]

As for the Church calendar, which presented a problem in so far as some of the Churches adhered to the old Julian calendar (which was thirteen days behind the Gregorian), it was decided that the Easter celebration, the date of which had been fixed by General Councils, must be celebrated by all Churches on the same Sunday according to the Julian style. As for the other festivals, the civil calendar of the particular country of each Church was to be followed.

In the fourth place, the Conference gave a great deal of attention to the ecumenical movement, particularly to the question as to whether to accept or reject the invitation to attend the Assembly of the World Council of Churches at Amsterdam. Of the number of speeches delivered on this subject, the one by the Russian Archpriest G. I. Razumovsky was biased and denunciatory, while that of Exarch Stephan was fairly appreciative and friendly in tone. But both these speakers, and others who dealt with the subject, agreed that the meetings at Oxford and Edinburgh in 1937 had completely changed the character of the movement by abandoning discussions of the doctrinal basis of ecumenism, and by merging the two previous movements — the Faith and Order and Life and Work — into one, the World Council of Churches. This latter body was declared to be a predominantly Protestant body, the membership of which extended even to such communions as deny all sacraments altogether, even the baptism and the holy communion. Razumovsky further denounced the World Council as having been engineered and financed by the 'Mason-Methodist' John R. Mott for the purpose of establishing 'a Universal Protestant collective Vatican.' [56] No wonder, then, that the plenary session adopted a Resolution which asserts that the World Council of Churches aims at becoming a politically-oriented, capitalistic 'Ecumenical Church': 'The directing of their efforts into the main stream of social and political life, and to the creating of an "Ecumenical Church" as an important international power, appear to be, as it were, a falling into that temptation which was rejected by Christ in the desert . . .' [57] This 'Ecumenical Church' is declared to be 'an institution within the State, which is in one way or another tied to it and which possesses secular influence.' In conclusion, the Resolution categorically asserts 'that all the Orthodox National Churches, which are participating in the present Conference, are obliged to refuse to take any part in the ecumenical movement in its present-day shape.' [58] Again one can discern the cloven hoof of the Soviet anti-Western and particularly anti-American propaganda sticking out of the decorously trousered ecclesiastical leg.

Finally, the Conference adopted 'An Appeal to the Christians of the Whole World,' drafted by Exarch Stephan of Bulgaria, in which the political overtones plainly predominate over the religious ones. It is not difficult to recognize that although the voice is that of the ecclesiastical

Jacob, the hands are plainly those of the Soviet Esau. The appeal declares:

Whereas the Orthodox East is inspired by the great principles of peace on earth and mutual brotherly love among men, the aggressiveness of the Western capitalist and imperialist world is only too strikingly obvious. It is from these that the danger of a new war with its unheard of terror for long-suffering mankind again approaches . . . We ministers of the Orthodox Church are made painfully anxious by the fact that the instigators of a new war are children of the Christian world — Catholic and Protestant. We grieve deeply that instead of hearing the voice of peace and Christian love from the fortress of Catholicism — the Vatican — and from that nest of Protestantism — America — we hear blessings bestowed on a new war and hymns of praise to atom bombs and similar inventions intended for the extermination of human life.

We sincerely pray and most ardently desire that in the love of God and one's neighbour, the pride and ambitions of the Vatican and those who support it may melt; so also that the self-confidence of Protestant rationalism should be replaced by Christian humility, in order that they (both Catholics and Protestants) may say in the words of St. Paul, 'By the grace of God I am what I am.' [59]

Although these resolutions were signed by the majority of the members of the conference and therefore presumably represent the common mind of the leaders of Eastern Orthodoxy, it is most significant to note that the representatives of the Constantinopolitan and the Greek Churches, although present, did not take part in the deliberations or the signing of the conclusions. Moreover, another Greek-dominated Church, that of Jerusalem, sent no delegates at all. Of course, all Russian churches abroad not subject to Moscow likewise were not present. The Constantinopolitan and the Greek Churches were officially censured for their non-co-operation: the Conference 'deeply regrets that the

hierarchs of the Greek Churches did not receive any author-
ity from their Heads, and first of all from His Holiness the
Ecumenical Patriarch, to participate in our Conference.' [60]
Moreover, the Greek, Alexandrian, Antiochene, and the
Constantinopolitan Churches not only attended the Second
Assembly of the World Council of Churches in Evanston
(1954) but their representatives were elected members of
the central committee, while Archbishop Michael of the
Greek Orthodox Archdiocese of North and South America
is one of its Presidents. Why did the Greek Churches abstain
from the deliberations at Moscow? This is a clear indication of the growing rift between them and the rest of the
autocephalous Churches which are obviously succumbing
to the leadership of Moscow. In fact, even at the Conference itself the Serbian Patriarch Gavrilo found it necessary
to deny categorically the current rumors that 'the Slav
Orthodox Churches, headed by the Russian Church,' are
'political tools of the Soviet Union.' And further, 'that the
Russian Orthodox Church is striving to subjugate to its
jurisdiction all the other National Orthodox Churches.' [61]

It may be safely asserted that the Moscow Conference of
1948 did not fall far short of being a Pan-Orthodox gathering, thus approximating in character the Eighth Ecumenical Council. Patriarch Alexei secured there recognition as
the *de facto* head of Eastern Orthodoxy. It has been ru-
mored that this is not the last such Conference, and that the
next one will have for its objective the *de jure* recognition
of Alexei or his successor as the Ecumenical Patriarch, and
the subjection of Eastern Orthodoxy to Russian hegemony.
Such an outcome is by no means fantastic or visionary.
When one considers that of the four ancient patriarchates,
two (Jerusalem and Antioch) are dependent on the subsidy
which the Soviet regime pays them (even though the Jerusa-

lem patriarchate refused to co-operate in 1948), and that, with the exception of the Greek autocephalous Churches, the majority of the others are likewise under the direct Moscow influence — some of them practically captives — then the possibility or feasibility of the plan becomes apparent. The Greek Churches are numerically small — the largest being the Orthodox Church of Greece. The Slavic churches are already in the majority and are augmented by several of the non-Slavic and non-Greek varieties. Accordingly, the ambitious plan of the Moscow patriarchate — with the support of the Soviet government — is quite practicable and realizable.

No wonder that when the Amsterdam Assembly actually organized the World Council of Churches, the judgment about this body expressed in the official *Journal of the Moscow Patriarchate* was severely condemnatory. Archpriest Razumovsky, who seems to be regarded as an expert on the subject, published an article [62] in which he ridiculed the Amsterdam Assembly and unblushingly twisted some of its declarations to prove that the whole movement was supported by the Riverside Church and Wall Street. He was particularly sarcastic about the role of the Council as a second Moses, saving the world from the impending catastrophe.

All aim at one goal — to force from God the repetition of the miracle, to enable Moses [i.e. the Church] to part the waters of the sea and make a dry passage; then to lead the hard-hearted Pharaoh into the sea and to drown his might in the waters of the Red Sea . . .'

He had this to say about John Foster Dulles's speech:

The circles of Mr. Dulles decided to establish an universal organization, i.e. the World Council of Churches, which would disorganize the growing unity of the world's political rebirth.

What a strange order for the Church! And at the same time anonymous!

He furthermore protests against the 'declaration of religious freedom' adopted by the Council, objecting that not *everyone* has the right to profess his faith, but only 'the apostles, teachers of the Church.'

Forgotten were even the most ancient canons, apostolic as well as conciliar, which once had been valid for all Christendom. Apostle John forbids communion with those differing in the faith. The canons forbid communion with those who were declared heretics and schismatics by the Church. But Amsterdam permits (par. 3) communion in religious matters *of all with all.*

The only good word he has to say about Amsterdam is given to the speech of J. L. Hromádka (whom he calls Hromadko), in which the Czech theologian declared that the West is already bankrupt.

The 'rumors' of the ambitious 'Moscow-the-Third-Rome' aspirations of Patriarch Alexei continued to flourish and were augmented by several incidents which gave color to them. Thus, for instance, when in 1949 Archbishop Athenagoras became Patriarch of Constantinople and sent Alexei a fraternal message offering restoration of friendly relations between the two Churches, the latter cold-shouldered the offer.[63] A few months later the official *Journal of the Moscow Patriarchate* published a sharp attack of Metropolitan Seraphim on the patriarchate of Constantinople, declaring that Moscow was the real center of Orthodoxy and deriding the title 'Ecumenical,' borne by Patriarch Athenagoras as devoid of significance.[64]

A similar instance of conflict between the two sees is to be seen in the article published in 1949 in the Moscow *Journal* under the title 'A Senseless Attack.' [65] The author,

A. Ivanov, there replies to a Greek, T. Papajannopoulos, who dared to affirm in the journal of the Patriarchate of Constantinople that the Patriarchate of Jerusalem is in imminent danger from the Russians. Ivanov answers in a tone of injured innocence, as if the idea were utterly preposterous and unjust:

It is difficult to tell [he writes] for what circle of readers the above-mentioned aspersion is intended. Not a single one of the Orthodox inhabitants, not only of Palestine but of the entire East, beginning with the hierarchs and ending with the ranks of the faithful, agrees with an assertion of that sort.

Really? Why was it necessary, then, for Patriarch Gavrilo to deny it? Or for Ivanov to answer it? Moreover, why is the Greek author a 'politician-phanariot,' while Mr. Ivanov and the other Russian churchmen are as innocent of politics as new-born lambs?

VII

It is evident from the resolutions of the Moscow Conference that the Russian Church had been given a political assignment comprising various propagandist objectives of the Soviet government, not the least of which is the so-called 'peace campaign.' The beginnings of it are traced to Premier Churchill's speech delivered at Fulton, Missouri, in 1947. Shortly afterwards Patriarch Alexei protested to Archbishop Damaskinos of Athens against the Greek civil war, 'in the face of which the Russian Orthodox Church can no longer keep silent.' The latter replied that the war was instigated by a communist minority.[66] From May 1949, the *Journal* has been full of 'peace' appeals, articles, and speeches. The Church has exerted herself to the utmost to mobilize the opinion of its faithful in behalf of 'peace.' The

Patriarch himself has made vigorous pronouncements in be-half of the campaign from time to time; thus in 1950 he sent out an appeal to the other Orthodox Churches, in which he urged them to combine in support of 'peace': 'It is time for all of us — pastors of Christ's flock — to declare openly so that all can hear that international problems must never again be decided by the destruction of millions of lives . . .' [67] But for the greatest part, Alexei has delegated Metropolitan Nikolai to this particular duty. Thus, for instance, it has been the latter who has served as the official delegate of the Russian Orthodox Church at the various in-ternational congresses held for this purpose. According to his own detailed, and by no means modest, description of the ovation which he received at the First World Congress of the Partisans of Peace (Paris, April 1949), where 2000 delegates were gathered, allegedly representing six million people all over the world (or so he reported), his part at the meeting was by no means negligible:

My speech was interrupted several times by an applause. When I concluded my speech (the last part of which I repeated in French), the whole assembly, with the presidium at the head, stood up, and there broke out anew a stormy ovation which the president could not still for a long while.[68]

At the Stockholm Peace Congress, the Russian declaration condemning atomic warfare was followed by similar decla-rations by the Churches of Bulgaria, Rumania, Albania, Poland, and others. In 1950, Nikolai was again the center of respectful attention when he attended a Conference of the Czechoslovak clergy of all denominations at Luhačovice. He is pictured in a snapshot walking arm in arm with Dean Hewlett Johnson of Canterbury. A similar conference, of which Metropolitan Nikolai was chairman, was held two years later in Moscow, where the head of every religious body in the USSR delivered a fervent speech in defense of peace. Of course, this was too good an opportunity not to put in a few words of denunciation of the American and British 'war-mongers!' [69]

Probably the severest denunciation of the United States to be found in any of the current Russian 'religious' publications is a speech by Metropolitan Nikolai delivered at one of the peace conferences. His language leaves nothing to be desired by the most rabid of the official Soviet 'hate-America' propagandists:

'Freedom' is sung by the sirens beyond the ocean. But only a man of black conscience and beclouded judgment is capable of talking about genuine freedom in a country where people are lynched, where children are kidnapped, where tear bombs are thrown among the workers, that is, among people who create the country's wealth, where bread is burned up before the eyes of the famished, where those people who attempt to give the term 'freedom' its authentic meaning are thrown into prisons, where gold is used for the bribing of those abroad who would co-operate with them, and where guns are cast so that the peaceful valleys of Greece, China, Indonesia, and Vietnam would be laved in human blood! Freedom to steal, to subjugate, to kill—such is their 'freedom'! [70]

And after quoting an irresponsible statement from the *Times-Herald* (Washington, 4 July 1949), Nikolai comments:

. . . that is not merely beastly, because animals having fed, are sated. But there is no limit to the devourings of the present-day cannibals. Traders in human blood and manufacturers of death, sitting on their bags of gold, they would be ready not only to destroy two hundred million of Soviet citizens, but all people everywhere . . .

Surely, no comment is necessary.

Although Nikolai has borne the brunt of the 'peace

campaigns,' Patriarch Alexei has not by any means stood aside from this kind of pro-Soviet politics. He exhorted a number of times the heads of all the Orthodox Churches to support the 'peace' proposals put forth by the Russian government, and to sign the Stockholm Peace Petition. In August 1950, he held a conference with the patriarchs of the Georgian and Armenian Churches in Tbilisi to find ways and means to stop the 'war-mongers' stubbornly 'preparing for war.' The three then issued a call to the entire Christendom to work for 'peace.' [71] In July 1951, on the occasion of the six-hundredth anniversary of the founding of the Trinity-Sergei monastery, Alexei invited to it the heads of the Antiochene, Georgian, Bulgarian, and Rumanian Churches, and they again issued a call to the world for peace. When the Korean War broke out, Alexei sent a protest to the Security Council of the United Nations against this 'American aggression.' 'The Russian Orthodox Church decisively condemns this interference and the resulting inhuman annihilation of the peaceful population of Korea by American aviation.' [72]

VIII

In conclusion, then, what is one to think about His Holiness, Alexei, Patriarch of Moscow and All Russia? To form a just opinion of him, in the light of his record, is indeed a very difficult task; nor dare I pronounce a judgment, gladly leaving all absolute judgments to Him Who sees into the hearts of men. And yet, that does not preclude a relative, professedly fallible estimate, an attempt at evaluation.

At best, Patriarch Alexei appears to be a hierarch sincerely loyal to the interests of his Church, whose exceedingly onerous and dangerous task it is to stand at her administrative helm during this extremely difficult period of her history. He is likewise a loyal citizen of the USSR, honestly convinced that the regime of the country is on the whole right in its civil policy, even though its ecclesiastical policy is affected by its anti-religious bias. So believing, he is deliberately paying a heavy, personal price in order to obtain, from a religiously unfriendly government the best terms and conditions of her existence he is able to secure. Whatever he is doing is for the best interests of the Church. He derives sanction for it from his honestly held belief that it is a Christian duty to submit to the government of his country, no matter what it might be, in accordance with the Apostle's solemn command: 'Let every soul be subject to higher powers. For there is no power but of God: the powers that be are ordained of God.' [73] And he can point, in support of his policy, to the marked revival of religious interest in Russia, as is witnessed by Harrison E. Salisbury,[74] who has recently returned from the Soviet Union after a five-year residence there. Salisbury reports that many churches have been reopened and are crowded with worshipers; that among them are many young people, and even communists; and that the government, despite a token anti-religious campaign, has apparently concluded that the Church presents no political danger. This amelioration of the situation is further emphasized by the Central Committee's decree, signed by Nikita S. Krushchev and published in November 1954, in *Pravda*.[75] In it the powerful leader of the Communist Party condemns attacks on the Church and admits 'gross mistakes' in the 'scientific atheistic propaganda.' Although the Party still calls for 'liberation' of the people from 'religious prejudices,' it cautions against over-zealous and offensive methods of carrying out this policy. As a token of this amelioration, seven additional churches were opened in Moscow, so that their number in January 1955 reached fifty-five.[76] All this goes to strengthen Alexei's policy.

The Patriarch further justifies his course by two mistaken considerations: first, the freedom of cult is erroneously regarded as complete freedom of religion, as we understand the term in the West. Liturgical and sacramental rites are identified with genuine religious liberties, and the Soviet government sedulously insists on keeping this error intact. The Church accepts this fatal limitation of its influence and restricts its activity accordingly. In the second place, the Russian Church has always identified itself with the nation as a whole, and does so now. This religious nationalism, the besetting sin of all Orthodox nations, works havoc with the religious character of the Church, particularly where the government and the large part of the nation are professedly irreligious or anti-religious. Thus Alexei sees in every service to the nation, i.e. the Soviet government, a service to God. Nevertheless, no matter how favorably or leniently one tries to evaluate the Patriarch's policy, it still leaves a large number of difficult questions unanswered.

At worst, the Patriarch is a careerist, co-operating with the government because he is thus able to exercise great, although limited, power. He knows that 'freedom of action' is possible only *within* the limits of the governmental policies, and he accepts these limitations. Even so, his personal ambition to make himself and the Russian Church supreme over all other Eastern Orthodox Churches has already been largely realized, thanks to the fact that it subserves the aims of the Soviet government as well. To reach this goal, he does not scruple to resort to the morally questionable or even reprehensible means of which his opponents accuse him. He has made himself and his Church a tool of the Soviet policy. His services to the state, as summarized by Professor Schmemann of the St. Vladimir Russian Orthodox Seminary in New York, comprise (1) 'resanctifying the state in the eyes of the West'; (2) 'conspicuous participation . . . in the "world peace" campaigns'; and (3) struggle against Roman Catholicism and the West.'[1]

Probably the truth lies somewhere between these two extremes, for human motives are mixed and rarely consistent. To accept the first hypothesis is far too simple and unrealistic; to maintain the second without reservations is to ignore the undeniably difficult position Patriarch Alexei occupies. One can neither exculpate him from wrong nor condemn him outright.

No matter what opinion we arrive at regarding the Patriarch, the fact remains that the Russian Church is subjugated by the state and exploited as a tool for the latter's far-ranging policies. But so it was under the tsars. The great difference is that the state now aims at eliminating all 'religious prejudices' from the Russian society and ultimately from the world. Despite the temporary adoption of tactics consciously designed to mask this intention and to lull the Russian believers and Christians of the world into a false sense of security, its final goal remains unchanged. The only hope which Christians may entertain is derived, in the first place, from the faith that all evil is self-destructive, and therefore that the Soviet evil is no more permanent than the tsarist evil was; secondly, from the possibility that the Soviet leaders may realize that without morality no worthy society or culture can be built, and may turn to the Church to obtain it; and thirdly, from the fact that despite the subservience of its sycophantic hierarchy, the rank and file of the believers have always lived their reli-

gious life apart from, and often in opposition to, their
official leaders, and therefore a similar situation may emerge
under the Soviets. Although the present regime is far more
dangerous to the religious life of its citizens than the tsarist
rule was, particularly because of the greater control over
the education of the younger generation, we must still trust
that the religious faith of the Russian people shall ultimately prove victorious. There always will be a 'holy
Russia.'

NOTES

[1] *Patriarkh Sergii i ego dukhovnoe nasledstvo* (Moscow, 1947), 50.
[2] Ibid. 282.
[3] Metropolitan Evlogy, *Put' moei zhizni* (Paris, Y.M.C.A. Press, 1947), 181.
[4] M. Polsky, *Kanonicheskoe polozhenie vysshei tserkovnoi vlasti v SSSR i zagranitsei* (Jordanville, N. Y., Holy Trinity Monastery, 1948), 98.
[5] Ibid. 98.
[6] *Chernaya kniga* (Paris, 1925), 259.
[7] *Patriarkh Sergii*, 283.
[8] *Patriarkh Sergii*, 135-6; also *Zhurnal* (1944), No. 6; *New York Times*, 22 May 1944.
[9] *Zhurnal* (1944), No. 7.
[10] *Patriarkh Sergii*, 292.
[11] Ibid. 296.
[12] Ibid. 301.
[13] *Zhurnal* (1944), No. 1.
[14] *Zhurnal* (1945), No. 2; English translation in *Orthodox Church Bulletin* (London, March 1945), 1-3.
[15] *Orthodox Church Bulletin* (London, March 1945), 3.
[16] Alexander Schmemann, 'The Church in Soviet Russia,' in *Proceedings of the Conference of the Institute for the Study of the History and Culture of the USSR* (New York, 1953), 97.
[17] N. S. Timasheff, 'Urbanization, Operation Anti-religion, and the Decline of Religion in the USSR' in *The American Slavic and East European Review* (New York, April 1955), 228.
[18] John S. Curtiss, *The Russian Church and the Soviet State* (Bos-

ton, 1953), 9–10. These figures are based on the official report of the Ober-Procurator of the Holy Synod for 1914.

[19] R. P. Casey, *Religion in Russia* (New York, 1946), 93.

[20] *Zhurnal* (1945), No. 5.

[21] Curtiss, op. cit. 308.

[22] *Zhurnal* (1954), No. 1.

[23] Curtiss, op. cit. 305.

[24] *Russie et Chrétienté* (1949), 149–53.

[25] *Patriarkh Sergii*, 351.

[26] Ibid. 352.

[27] Ibid. 345.

[28] Ibid. 346.

[29] Ibid. 347.

[30] Ibid. 348.

[31] It is fully described in *Orthodox Church Bulletin* (London, July 1945).

[32] *Zhurnal* (1945), No. 11.

[33] *Zhurnal* (1946), No. 2.

[34] Joseph Dzvonchik, 'My Journey to Moscow,' in *The Russian Orthodox Journal* (September 1945), 13.

[35] N. S. Timasheff, 'The Moscow Council and the Russian Orthodox Church in America,' in *The Russian Orthodox Journal* (March 1946). Also see *New York Times*, 8 April 1945.

[36] *The Russian Orthodox Journal* (February 1947), 7.

[37] *Zhurnal* (1948), No. 1.

[38] *New York Times*, 18 March 1946.

[39] *Zhurnal of the Moscow Patriarchate* (1948), No. 10.

[40] *New York Times*, 7, 13, 19 March 1946; and 15 April 1946.

[41] *Zhurnal* (1949), No. 10; also 1950, No. 7.

[42] Matthew Spinka, 'The Religious Situation in Czechoslovakia,' in *Czechoslovakia*, Robert J. Kerner, ed. (Berkeley and Los Angeles, 1940), 296.

[43] *Zhurnal* (1946), No. 1.

[44] *Zhurnal* (1946), No. 8.

[45] *Zhurnal* (1945), No. 9.

[46] Nikolai Pop, *Kirche unter Hammer und Sichel* (Berlin, 1953), 38.

[47] *Zhurnal* (1946), No. 11.

[48] *Zhurnal* (1947), No. 3.

[49] *Zhurnal* (1947), No. 11.

[50] Pop, op. cit. 50, 127; *Zhurnal* (1950), Nos. 7 and 9.

[51] S. P., *O tserkvi v SSSR* (Paris, 1947).

[52] *Major Portions of the Proceedings of the Conference of Heads and Representatives of Autocephalous Orthodox Churches in Connection with the Celebration of 500 years of Autocephaly of the Russian Orthodox Church* (Paris, YMCA Press, 1952), 129.

[53] *The Proceedings*, 237.

[54] Cf. Schmemann, 'The Church in Soviet Russia,' op. cit. 98.

[55] *The Proceedings*, 239.

[56] Ibid. 168–9.

[57] Ibid. 240.

[58] Ibid. 241.

[59] Ibid. 247.

[60] Ibid. 248.

[61] Ibid. 246.

[62] *Zhurnal* (1949), No. 5.

[63] Ibid.

[64] *Zhurnal* (1949), No. 12.

[65] *Zhurnal* (1954), No. 6.

[66] Quoted in Curtiss, op. cit. 317.

[67] *Zhurnal* (1950), No. 3.

[68] *Mitropolit Nikolai, Slova i rechi* (Moscow, 1950), II, 311.

[69] *Conference in Defense of Peace of All Churches and Religious Associations in the USSR* (Moscow Patriarchate, 1952). This book was translated and published in four other languages besides the Russian.

[70] *Mitropolit Nikolai, Slova*, 318.

[71] *Zhurnal* (1950), No. 3.

[72] *Zhurnal* (1950), No. 5.

[73] Romans, 13:1.

[74] *New York Times*, 29 Sept. 1954; also his *American in Russia* (New York, 1955).

[75] *New York Times*, 12 Nov. 1954.

[76] *New York Times*, 7 Jan. 1955.

[77] Schmemann, 'The Church in Soviet Russia,' op. cit. 97.

APPENDIX I

LETTER of Metropolitan Sergei of Nizhni Novgorod to the Bishops, Priests, and Faithful of the Patriarchate of Moscow.

Nizhni Novgorod
May 28/June 10, 1926

One of the matters of constant concern to our late Patriarch was the legal recognition of the Patriarchal Orthodox Church and thereby of the possibility of a lawful existence in the territory of the USSR.

To be sure, our parishes possess full rights of existence (in accordance with their agreements with the government), and as such have the right to recognize at will their superiors in purely spiritual questions. Consequently, the Orthodox hierarchy, in its contacts with the parishes, in holding itself exclusively within the canonical limits, and in not claiming any administrative function or formal jurisdiction, acts within the framework of the law. Nevertheless, the lack of a special registration on the part of our Church's directing bodies creates for the hierarchy many practical difficulties which impart to its activity a somewhat hidden or even conspiratorial appearance, which in turn gives rise to a number of misunderstandings and suspicions.

With the view to remedy such a situation, and following in this matter the example of the Most Holy Patriarch, I addressed myself to the Peoples' Commissariat of Internal Affairs to secure the registration of our ecclesiastical administration. Today I have the pleasure of informing you that the government has acceded to my request. Having received these rights, we owe obligations to the power from which these rights emanate.

I have likewise taken it upon myself, in the name of our entire Orthodox hierarchy and of our flock, to declare before the Soviet Power our sincere will to be citizens fully respecting the laws of the Soviet Union; to be loyal toward its government; and to hold ourselves absolutely apart from all political parties and enterprises which could harm the Union.

But let us be sincere to the end. We cannot pass over in silence the contradictions which exist between our Orthodox [people] and the communists who govern our Union. The latter struggle against God and His rule in the hearts of the people, while we see the significance and aim of our entire existence in the confession of faith in God as well as in the widest dissemination and affirmation of that faith in peoples' hearts. They accept exclusively the materialistic conception of history, while we believe in divine Providence, in miracles, etc.

Far from promising reconciliation of that which is irreconcilable and from pretending to adapt our faith to communism, we will remain from the religious point of view what we are, i.e. members of the traditional Church.

We do not see the progress of our Church in an adaptation of the Church to 'modern exigencies,' nor in the mutilation of its ideals, nor in a modification of its doctrine or canons, but in the success of our endeavor to rekindle and conserve, under present conditions, and in all its purity, the habitual fire of faith and love of God in the hearts of our flock: so that the faithful may learn, at the zenith of material progress, to see the true significance of life beyond the grave, rather than here below.

We are persuaded, in other respects, that the Orthodox Christian who guards his faith sacredly and lives in accordance with its precepts, will for this very reason be a useful and exemplary citizen in whatever state, including the Soviet state, [he may live, and] in every aspect of his social relations: whether it be in factory, in village and city, in the army or in the mine. Should the state require renunciation of property, or giving his life for the common good, should he be required to give an example of temperance, honesty, or zeal in society — that is precisely what Christians are taught by their faith to do.

In any case, since not only the communists, but also men of religious faith, are regarded as citizens of the Soviet Union, every Orthodox Christian can claim his place among them (for he represents the overwhelming majority of the population).

But while promising complete loyalty obligatory upon all citizens of the Union, we, representatives of the ecclesiastical hierarchy, cannot enter into any special engagement to prove our loyalty. We cannot accept, for example, the duty of watching over the political tendencies of our co-religionists, even if such surveillance were to be limited to guaranteeing the political security of some and to depriving others of that guarantee. The Soviet government disposes of much more adequate organs and much more efficient means for that purpose.

Above all, we cannot exercise executive functions or resort to ecclesiastical controls against elements little favorable to the Soviet power.

One of the results of the Revolution consists in the freeing of the Church from all political and national tasks, and we assuredly cannot surrender that advantage. Besides, the faithful would not pardon us if we renounced it. But we firmly promise that to the degree it depends on our authority, we will not henceforth permit the Church to find itself involved in any political adventure whatsoever, and will not tolerate anyone to hide his own political aspirations under the Church's name.

We are asked here to state precisely our point of view concerning the Russian clergy who left in the wake of the *émigrés* abroad, where they established a kind of affiliated Russian Church. Since they do not consider themselves citizens of the Soviet Union, and do not regard themselves as in any way concerned with the Soviet government, members of the clergy abroad permit themselves, on occasion, to engage in hostile manifestations against the Union. Responsibility for it falls on the entire Russian Church continuing to exist in the territories of the Soviet Union of which its members are citizens, along with all the consequences following therefrom.

To inflict ecclesiastical punishment on clerical *émigrés* guilty of unfaithfulness toward the Soviet Union would not produce the desired effect and might offer new proof to the allegations that such decisions had been forced on us by the Soviet government. The only thing that appears to us desirable and perfectly feasible is to assert our complete disavowal of such political clergy, and to repudiate in advance all responsibility

for their political action. To that end it suffices to establish
the rule that all members of the clergy who do not acknowledge their civil obligation toward the Soviet Union ought to
be excluded from the ecclesiastical community of the Moscow
patriarchate and ought to place themselves under the jurisdiction of the Orthodox Churches in the countries where they
reside.

These same obligations ought to condition the existence
abroad of the administrative ecclesiastical organs such as the
Holy Synod and the diocesan councils.

Being thus separated from the *émigrés,* we shall build our
Church's life within the territories of the USSR free from all
politics, although mindful of our civil duty toward the Soviet
Union that has sheltered us and has legalized our existence.

I call upon all Orthodox bishops to make this appeal known
to their dioceses and ask them to inform me of the reaction
thereto.

In behalf of the Patriarchate
Sergei, Metropolitan of Nizhni Novgorod

Appendix II

Declaration of Metropolitan Sergei, addressed to the Pastors and the Flock, and dated July 16/29, 1927.

By the Grace of God!

The humble Sergei, Metropolitan of Nizhni Novgorod, deputy Guardian of the Patriarchate, with the temporary patriarchal Holy Synod — to the most reverend archpastors, God-loving pastors, honored monks, and to all faithful members of the Holy All-Russian Church; rejoice in the Lord!

Among the cares of our late most holy father, Patriarch Tikhon, before his death, was the placing of our Russian Church in a legalized relation to the Soviet government and thus securing for the Church the possibility of a fully legal and peaceful existence. Dying, the Patriarch exclaimed: 'I would need to live another three short years!' And indeed, if the unexpected demise had not cut short his holy labors, he would have carried this undertaking to its completion. Unfortunately, various circumstances, and principally the activities of the enemies of the Soviet government abroad, among whom were found not only the rank and file of the faithful of our Church, but their leaders as well, and which aroused on the part of the government a just distrust against all Church functionaries, hampered his efforts. Thus it was not granted him to see his efforts completed during his life.

Now that the lot of being the temporary vicar of the Primate of our Church has fallen on me, the unworthy Metropolitan Sergei, it has also become my duty to continue the efforts of the deceased in striving by all means to bring about a peaceful ordering of our Church affairs. My efforts in this direction, shared with me by the Orthodox archpastors, have not remained fruitless; with the establishment of the temporary Holy Synod, the hope for bringing into proper state and order all of our ecclesiastical administration has been strengthened, and confidence in the possibility of peaceful life and activity within the limits of law has been increased. Now, when we are almost at the very goal of our efforts, the provocative acts of our enemies abroad still continue: murders, arsons, airplane flights, explosions, and other similar occurrences of underground war are plainly seen by us all. These acts disturb the peaceful tenor of life, create an atmosphere of mutual distrust, and all manner of suspicion. Hence, it is so much more needful for our Church, and therefore the duty of all of us to whom her interests are dear, who desire to bring her on the road of legalized and peaceful existence, to show that we, as Church functionaries, are not enemies of our Soviet government and do not participate in these senseless intrigues, but are at one with our nation and our government.

To manifest these sentiments is the first goal of our present task (mine and the Synod's). Therefore, we wish to inform you that in May of the current year, upon my request and with the permission of the government, we organized the temporary Holy Synod to assist the deputy Guardian (of the Patriarchate). It is composed of the undersigned members. There are still absent the Most Reverend Metropolitan Arseny of Novgorod, who has not yet arrived, and the Archbishop Sebastian of Kostroma, who is ill. Our endeavor to secure the permission for the Synod to begin its task of administering the Orthodox All-Russian Church has been crowned with success.

At present our Orthodox Church in the Union possesses not only canonical, but also fully legal, centralized administration consonant with civil laws. We furthermore hope that this legalization will be gradually extended to the lower ecclesiastical administrations: archdiocesan, regional, etc. Is it necessary to enlarge upon the significance of the consequences of the change that has occurred in the status of our Orthodox Church, of her clergy, and all her functionaries and institutions?

Let us raise our grateful prayers to the Lord who has been so gracious to our holy Church. Let us also express, in behalf of the entire nation, our gratitude to the Soviet government for this attention to the spiritual needs of the Orthodox population, and at the same time let us assure the government that we will not abuse its confidence reposed in us.

Addressing ourselves, with God's blessing, to our synodal

labors, we clearly realize the magnitude of our task that lies
not only before us but before all Church leaders. We need to
show not in words, but in deeds, that not only people in-
different to Orthodoxy, or those who reject it, may be faithful
citizens of the Soviet Union, loyal to the Soviet government, but
likewise the most fervent adherents of Orthodoxy, to whom
it is as precious with all its canonical and liturgical treasures
as truth and life. We wish to remain Orthodox and at the same
time to recognize the Soviet Union as our civil fatherland
whose joys and successes are our joys and successes, and whose
misfortunes are our misfortunes. Every blow directed against
the Union, be it war, boycott, or any other common disaster,
or even a hole-and-corner murder as the one that occurred in
Warsaw, we acknowledge as a blow directed against us. Remaining Orthodox, we regard it our duty to be citizens of
the Union 'not from fear, but from conscience,' as the Apostle
has taught us (Rom. 13:5). And we are hopeful that with God's
help, by our mutual co-operation and support, we shall ac-
complish that task.

We may be hindered only in the way in which the establishment of the Church life on principles of loyalty had been
hindered during the first years of the Soviet rule, namely, by
an insufficient recognition of the seriousness of that which has
occurred in our country. Many people have misunderstood
the establishment of the Soviet regime, regarding it as a fortui-
tous event; hence, as something not binding upon them.

People have forgotten that for a Christian there are no for-
tuitous events, and that what has occurred in our land, as
everywhere and at all times, has been the work of God's providence, undeviatingly leading every nation toward its pre-
destined goal. To such people, refusing to recognize 'the signs
of the times,' to break with the former regime or even with the
monarchy without breaking with Orthodoxy, may appear impossible. Such an attitude, expressed in words and deeds by
certain ecclesiastical groups, has aroused the Soviet government's suspicion and has hindered the efforts of the holy
Patriarch to establish peaceful relations between the Church
and the Soviet government. Not in vain does the Apostle tell
us that we may live in godliness, 'quietly and peaceably,' only

if we submit to the lawful government (1 Tim. 2:2); otherwise, we ought to leave the community. Only arm-chair visionaries can suppose that such an immense community as our Orthodox Church, with all its organizations, may peacefully exist in this country, hiding itself from the government. Now when our patriarchate, fulfilling the will of the late Patriarch, has decisively and undeviatingly embarked on the path of loyalty, people of the above-mentioned tendencies must, turning about and leaving their own political sympathies behind, bring to the Church only their faith and work with us only in the name of that faith; or, if they cannot immediately make the change, they must at least cease to interfere with us, temporarily refraining from all activity. We are confident that they will again and very soon return to co-operation with us, having become convinced that the change has taken place only in our relation to the regime, while the faith and the Orthodox life remain unaltered.

The problem of the émigré clergy under these circumstances is especially poignant. The openly anti-Soviet actions of some archpastors and pastors, greatly detrimental to the relations between the government and the Church, have forced the late Patriarch, as is known, to depose the Synod abroad (April 23/ May 5, 1922). Nevertheless, the Synod has continued to exist hitherto, and has not changed its politics. Moreover, by its pretentions to rule, it has lately divided the ecclesiastical community abroad into two camps. In order to put an end to this state of affairs, we demanded from the clergy abroad a written promise of their complete loyalty to the Soviet government in all their public activities. Those who fail to make such a promise, or to observe it, shall be expelled from the ranks of the clergy subject to the Moscow patriarchate. We think that having set up such limits, we shall be secure against all unexpected happenings abroad. On the other hand, our demand may perhaps cause many to pause and consider whether the time has not come to revise their attitude toward the Soviet regime, so as not to be cut off from their native Church and land.

We deem it no less weighty a task to prepare and issue a call for the Second All-Russian Sobor which would choose no longer a temporary, but the permanent central Church administration and which would also deal with those 'usurpers of power' in the Church who are tearing the robe of Christ asunder. The order and the time of the call, the subjects of discussion of the Sobor, and all other details will be worked out later. We shall at present only express our firm conviction that the future Sobor, having solved many of the most painful problems of the Church's inner life, will at the same time give its final approval, with one mind and voice, to the task undertaken by us in establishing regular relations between our Church and the Soviet regime.

In conclusion, we earnestly pray you, most reverend arch-pastors, pastors, and brothers and sisters, each of you in his own station to help us with your sympathy in God's work, with your devotion and obedience to the holy Church, and par-ticularly with your prayers to the Lord for us, that He may grant us a successful and God-pleasing accomplishment of the work laid upon us, to the glory of His Holy Name, to the well-being of our holy Orthodox Church, and to our common salva-tion.

The Grace of Our Lord Jesus Christ, the love of God the Father, and the communion of the Holy Spirit be with you all. Amen.

Moscow, July 16/29, 1927.

In behalf of the Guardian of the Patriarchate:
Sergei, Metropolitan of Nizhni Novgorod

Members of the Temporary Patriarchial Holy Synod:

Seraphim, Metropolitan of Tver
Sylvester, Archbishop of Vologda
Alexei, Archbishop of Khytin, administering the
Novgorod archdiocese
Anatoly, Archbishop of Samara
Pavel, Archbishop of Vyatka
Filipp, Archbishop of Zvenigorod, administering
the Moscow archdiocese
Konstantin, Bishop of Sumy, administering the
Kharkov archdiocese
Sergei, Bishop of Serpukhov, executive secretary

Selected Bibliography

I. Works dealing principally with the period since 1917

Anderson, Paul B., *People, Church and State in Modern Russia* (New York, 1944).

Bates, M. Serle, *Religious Liberty* (New York, 1945).

Berdyaev, Nicolas, *Dream and Reality* (New York, 1950).

Bolshakoff, Serge, *Russian Nonconformity* (Philadelphia, 1950).

Casey, Robert Pierce, *Religion in Russia* (New York, 1946).

Church under Communism, The, Church of Scotland General Assembly (New York, 1953).

Cockburn, J. Hutchison, *Religious Freedom in Eastern Europe* (Richmond, Va., 1953).

Conference in Defense of Peace of All Churches and Religious Associations in the U.S.S.R. (Moscow, 1952).

Curtiss, John Shelton, *The Russian Church and the Soviet State, 1917–1950* (Boston, 1953).

———, *Church and State in Russia* (New York, 1940).

Deyaniya drugago vserossiiskago pomestnago Sobora 1923 goda (Moscow, 1923).

d'Herbigny, M., S.J., *Tserkovnaya zhizn v Moskve* (Paris, 1926).

Emhardt, W. C., *Religion in Soviet Russia* (Milwaukee, 1929).

Evlogy, Mitropolit, *Put' moei zhizni* (Paris, 1947).

Fedotov, G. P., *The Russian Church since the Revolution* (New York, 1928).

———, *I est i budet* (Paris, 1932).

Fioletov, N. N., *Tserkov i gosudarstvo po sovetskomu pravu* (Moscow, 1924).

Gidulyanov, P. V., *Otdelenie tserkvi ot gosudarstva v S.S.S.R.* (Moscow, 1926), 3rd ed.

Gsovski, V. ed., *Church and State behind the Iron Curtain* (New York, 1955).

Krasikov, P. A., *Na tserkovnom fronte, 1918–1923* (Moscow, 1923).

Lieb, Fritz, *Russland unterwegs* (Bern, 1945).

Lzhe-pravoslavie na podyemye (Jordanville, N. Y., 1954).

McCullagh, Francis, *The Bolshevist Persecution of Religion* (London, 1924).

MacEoin, Gary, *The Communist War on Religion* (New York, 1951).

Major Portions of the Proceedings of the Conference of the Heads of the Autocephalous Orthodox Churches, held in Moscow, July, 1948 (Paris, 1952).

Miliukov, P. N., *Outlines of Russian Culture* (Philadelphia, 1942), 3 Parts, Part I, *Religion and the Church*.

Nikolaev, K. N., *Vostochny obryad* (Paris, 1950).

Nikolai, Mitropolit, *Slova i rechi* (Moscow, 1950), vol. II.

O polozhenii pravoslavnoi tserkvi v sovyetskom soyuzye (Jordanville, N. Y., 1951).

Patriarkh Sergii i ego dukhovnoe nasledstvo (Moscow, 1947).

Polsky, M., *Kanonicheskoe polozhenie vysshei tserkovnoi vlasti v S.S.S.R. i zagranitsei* (Jordanville, N. Y., 1948).

Pravda o religii v Rossii (Moscow, 1942).

Rozhdestvensky, A. P., *Svateishy Tikhon, patriarkh Moskovsky i vseya Rossii* (Sofia, Bulgaria, n.d.).

Russkaya pravoslavnaya tserkov i velikaya otechestvennaya voina (Moscow, n.d.).

Sheen, Fulton J., *Communism and the Conscience of the West* (Indianapolis, 1948).

Spinka, Matthew, *The Church and the Russian Revolution* (New York, 1927).

——, *Christianity Confronts Communism* (New York, 1936; London, 1938).

——, *Nicolas Berdyaev: Captive of Freedom* (Philadelphia, 1950).

Stratonov, I., *Russkaya tserkovnaya smuta, 1921–1931* (Berlin, 1932).

Timasheff, Nicholas S., *Religion in Soviet Russia, 1917–1942* (New York, 1942).

——, *The Great Retreat* (New York, 1946).

Titlinov, B. V., *Novaya tserkov* (Petrograd, 1923).

——, *Tserkov vo vremya revolutsii* (Petrograd, 1924).

——, *Pravoslavie ve sluzhbe samoderzhaviya v russkom gosudarstve* (Leningrad, 1924).

Troitsky, S. V., *Chto sdelal patriarkh Tikhon dlya tserkvi i rodiny* (Odessa, 1919).

——, *Razmezhevanie ili raskol* (Paris, 1932).

Trubetskoy, G., *Krasnaya Rossiya i svataya Rus* (Paris, 1931).

Valentinov, A. A., *Chernaya kniga* (Paris, 1925).

Vvedensky, A., *Tserkov i gosudarstvo* (Moscow, 1923).

——, *Tserkov patriarkha Tikhona* (Moscow, 1923).

Vyshinsky, Andrei Y., ed., *The Law of the Soviet State* (New York, 1948).

Weiant, E. T., *Sources of Modern Mass Atheism in Russia* (privately printed).

Zaitsev, Kirill, *Pravoslavnaya tserkov v sovyetskoi Rossii* (Shanghai, 1947).

Zyzykin, M., *Tserkov i mezhdunarodnoe pravo* (Warsaw, 1938).

II. Periodicals

The American Slavic and East European Review, New York.

Antireligioznik, Moscow.

Ateist, Moscow.

Bezbozhnik, Moscow.

Bezbozhnik u stanka, Moscow.

Orthodox Life, Jordanville, N. Y.

Put', Paris.

Revolutsiya i tserkov, Moscow.

The Russian Review, New York.

Slavonic Review, London.

Zhurnal Moskovskoi Patriarkhii, Moscow.